To Ba[...]
Enjoy!
    from Susan

COURTESY VIRGINIA MILITARY INSTITUTE MUSEUM

STONEWALL JACKSON

STONEWALL
MEMORIES FROM THE RANKS

BY
ALLEN CHRISTIAN REDWOOD
AND OTHERS

SELECTED BY
SHORNE HARRISON

EDITED AND INTRODUCED BY
MARIAN AND DAVID NOVAK

**Signal Tree Publications
Livermore, Maine
and
Rockbridge Baths, Virginia**

Copyright © 1998
Signal Tree Publications

Published in 1998 by
Signal Tree Publications

POB 551   POB 48
Livermore   Rockbridge Baths
Maine 04253   Virginia 24473

All rights reserved by the publisher. Apart from what is considered fair use, no part of this book may be used or reproduced in any manner whatsoever without written permission of the publisher except for brief quotations in reviews or articles.

Printed and bound in the United States of America

ISBN 0-9651858-2-6

Logo drawn by Dorothy Blackwell

TO THE MEMORY OF
DENNIE DONALD PETERSON
2nd LIEUTENANT, USMC
17 MAY 1943 – 6 SEPTEMBER 1967
WHOSE UNDERSTANDING OF DUTY WOULD HAVE PLEASED STONEWALL . . .

A. C. REDWOOD

"His banner grew old and faded and shot-torn. His legions grew ragged and foot-sore and weary. No matter who hesitated, Jackson advanced. Fierce in the heat of battle, because it was his duty to kill. [But] when the roar of the cannon died away the groans of the wounded reached a heart [that] throbb[ed] with every groan."

– *A FEDERAL SOLDIER*

STONEWALL BRIGADE
FIRST DIVISION
SECOND CORPS
ARMY OF NORTHERN VIRGINIA
GENERAL ROBERT EDWARD LEE, COMMANDING

"... [A] private in the 18th North Carolina was killed [on June 30, 1862] charging an enemy position near the Glendale [C]rossroads. A Confederate officer recorded that the young man's regiment advanced shouting the battle cry 'Stonewall!'"

TABLE OF CONTENTS

INTRODUCTION

FOREWARD
    By Shorne Harrison   xv

JACKSON'S BELOVED, LAST HOME: "THE GRANARY
OF THE CONFEDERACY"   xix

ALLEN CHRISTIAN REDWOOD   xxvii
    By Shorne Harrison

PREFACE   xxxv
    By James Alexander Walker

PART I: TEACHER, HUSBAND, SOLDIER

THOMAS JONATHAN JACKSON   3
    By Shorne Harrison

JACKSON IN LEXINGTON   11
    By John Newton Lyle

STONEWALL JACKSON'S SCABBARD SPEECH   13
    By William Alexander Obenchain

ON THE WAY TO WAR   21
    By George Henry Moffett

PART II: THE WAR BEGINS

GENERAL THOMAS J. JACKSON   27
    By Dr. Hunter Holmes McGuire

JUNE 1861: JUST BEFORE MANASSAS   39
    By John Newton Lyle

LET OUR MEN SLEEP   41
    By John Newton Lyle & Colonel John T. L. Preston

PART III: "STONEWALL"

LIKE A STONE WALL   49

  By Anonymous

WHAT GENERAL BEE SAID AND DID   50
  By William M. Robins

THE STONEWALL BRIGADE   52
  By John Newton Lyle

STONEWALL JACKSON UNDER THE TABLE   54
  By Anonymous

ASLEEP IN A SECOND   55
  By Charles Minor Blackford

SKETCHES OF STONEWALL   56
  By Gideon Draper Camden

I WISH I COULD GO WITH HIM   58
  By Hugh Augustus White

JACKSON UP A TREE   61
  By John Newton Lyle

HARD MARCHING   62
  By Sam R. Watkins

STONEWALL JACKSON--A MEMORY   65
  By Allen Christian Redwood

IN THE SHENANDOAH VALLEY, 1862   77
  By Andrew Davidson Long

THE HERO OF THE VALLEY   83
  By William H. Andrews

JACKSON AT CLOSE RANGE   85
  By David Eldred Holt

THAT MAN JACKSON   86
  By H.M. Wharton

FOLLOW YOUR GENERAL, BOYS   88
  By Charles Minor Blackford

"STONEWALL JACKSON'S WAY" By John Williamson Palmer	90
WITH JACKSON'S "FOOT CAVALRY" AT THE SECOND MANASSAS By Allen Christian Redwood	92
JACKSON OR A RABBIT By Berry Greenwood Benson	118
UNCLE STONE WALL By James Thompson	121
JACKSON'S RAGGED REBELS By Anonymous	124
SUCH A LEADER By Viscount Garnet Wolseley	125
"HURRAH FOR JACKSON!" By The Liberty Hall Volunteers	129

PART IV: CHANCELLORSVILLE

LEE AND JACKSON By Walter A. Montgomery	132
WE COULD NOT CHEER By David Eldred Holt	136
THREE GENERALS AT CHANCELLORSVILLE By Andrew Davidson Long	137
TWO MEN ON CRACKER BOXES By James Power Smith	139
THE LAST TIME I SAW HIM By Allen Christian Redwood	142
"PRESS ON; PRESS ON" By Dr. Hunter McGuire	144
WHERE STONEWALL WAS WOUNDED By Alexander Tedford Barclay	145

THE BRIGADE MUST NOT KNOW Anonymous Poem	151
WE HAD LOST JACKSON By Berry Greenwood Benson	153
THIS IS CALLED THE BATTLE OF CHANCELLORSVILLE By George W. Koontz	154
THE DEATH OF JACKSON By John Overton Casler	161
IN HIS OLD SECTION ROOM By Samuel Baldwin Hannah	169
HONOR TO THE OLD HERO By Charles Thomas Haigh	172

PART V: EPILOGUE

SHORT *ONE* MAN By Allen Christian Redwood	176
LOSS AND SURRENDER By Walter Montgomery	177
THE OILCLOTH COAT By Joseph Bryan	178
A POEM By Mary Ashley Townsend	183
GOODBYE TO STONEWALL By Henry Kyd Douglas	186
A SHRINE IN THE VALLEY By Dr. Hunter McGuire	188
SELECTED BIBLIOGRAPHY	190
ENDNOTES	191
INDEX	202

ILLUSTRATIONS

STONEWALL JACKSON	ii
STONEWALL BRIGADE	v
NEAR LEXINGTON, VIRGINIA	xviii
JACKSON'S HOME IN THE VALLEY	xxii
STONEWALL JACKSON'S HEADQUARTERS	xxv
ALLEN CHRISTIAN REDWOOD	xxvi
BEHIND THE STONE WALL	xxviii
REDWOOD'S SELF PORTRAIT	xxix
CONFEDERATE ARTILLERY FIRING ON UNION COLUMNS	xxx
SAYING GOODBYE	xxxi
BARKSDALE'S MISSISSIPPIANS	xxxii
ON TO SHARPSBURG	xxxiv
STONEWALL	xxxvii
PROFESSOR MAJOR T.J. JACKSON, 1855	xxxviii
NEW RECRUIT	1
THOMAS JONATHAN JACKSON	2
JACKSON AT 24 YEARS	4
ELINOR JUNKIN JACKSON AND MAJOR THOMAS JACKSON	6
MARY ANNA JACKSON	8
GENERAL THOMAS JONATHAN JACKSON	9
LEXINGTON, VIRGINIA	10
VIRGINIA MILITARY INSTITUTE	14
A SECTION ROOM AT VMI	18
DRILLMASTERS FOR JACKSON	20
JACKSON'S OLD HAT	23
THOMAS J. JACKSON	24
ON THE MARCH	25
GOODBYE TO WASHINGTON COLLEGE	26
DR. HUNTER HOLMES McGUIRE	28
SOUTHERN GENERALS	37

GOING TO MANASSAS	45
MAJOR GENERAL THOMAS JONATHAN JACKSON	46
ON THE ATTACK	47
GENERAL JACKSON AT MANASSAS	51
JACKSON	53
SKETCHES OF STONEWALL JACKSON	57
CAPTAIN HUGH WHITE	59
FIRST NATIONAL FLAG OF THE CONFEDERACY	60
THE COLD SENTRY	64
VMI DRILL FIELD	67
UNDER ARTILLERY ATTACK	70
A.P. HILL	72
CROSSING THE RAPIDAN	74
BERDAN'S SHARPSHOOTERS	84
CAPTURED BY JACKSON HIMSELF!	94
JOINING JACKSON'S CORPS	96
SHORT RATIONS	101
SINEWS OF WAR	102
"WHAT A PRIZE IT WAS!"	106
JACKSON'S FOOT CAVALRY	107
A LOUISIANA PELICAN	110
"JACKSON IS COMING!"	117
STATUE OF BERRY BENSON	119
A TAR HEEL	122
RAGGED REBELS	124
STONEWALL JACKSON	126
JACKSON IN WINTER DRESS	128
STONEWALL	130
THE CANNONEER	131
A LOUISIANA TIGER	137
COUNCIL OF WAR	140
THE LAST MEETING	143
WOUNDED	147

CAMP TOILET	149
WOUNDING OF JACKSON	150
JACKSON'S STAFF	152
MEN OF STONEWALL'S CORPS AT HAMILTON'S CROSSING	155
CHANCELLORSVILLE	158
STONEWALL JACKSON	160
MAJOR HAWKS	163
GUINEA STATION	165
THE STAINLESS BANNER	168
VMI CADETS AT STONEWALL JACKSON'S GRAVE	171
CHARLES THOMAS HAIGH	173
T.J. JACKSON	174
TO THE REAR	175
THE OILCLOTH COAT	181
JULIA JACKSON	185
OUR STONEWALL	187
NEAR LEXINGTON, VIRGINIA	188
JACKSON STATUE AT RICHMOND	Back Cover

MAPS

SHENANDOAH VALLEY	xxiii
TO MANASSAS	40
FIRST MANASSAS	48
THE VALLEY	78-79
WINCHESTER	81
CEDAR MOUNTAIN TO SECOND MANASSAS	99
THE MARYLAND CAMPAIGN	123
FREDERICKSBURG TO CHANCELLORSVILLE	134-135

FOREWARD

Years ago, in a small store on the road to the Chancellorsville battlefield, I paused after making a purchase to ask the woman behind the counter a question. I had just come from the tiny, deserted cemetery where the amputated left arm of Stonewall Jackson lies buried beneath a simple granite marker, and I was puzzled. "Why is it," I wanted to know, "that when arms and legs lay in bloody piles beneath first-floor windows of every building used as a hospital during the Civil War, they bothered to bury Stonewall Jackson's arm?" The woman's response was fiercely immediate, though softly spoken: "Because every little bit of him was precious."

I think there can be little doubt that Stonewall Jackson was a legend in his own time. In these pages you will find words about him not only from memoirs written in later years when legend had grown to the magnitude of myth, but from varied contemporary sources as well: newspaper accounts from the North, South, and overseas; soldiers' letters written by both Rebel and Yankee; homefront diaries; and official documents (including the very unlikely TENTH ANNUAL REPORT OF THE SUPERINTENDENT OF COMMON SCHOOLS OF THE STATE OF MAINE!).

It is impossible to say how much of the information that has come down to us regarding Jackson is absolutely reliable. Sometimes personal accounts conflict with one another or with newspaper reports; the newspaper reports do not agree with the official reports; and the official reports do not match the facts as we know them today. Still, what has come down to us about General Thomas Jonathan "Stonewall" Jackson is a body of material that, when taken as a whole, hangs together well--often even the discrepancies are explained--so that we can know much about who and what he was.

When we search for truth among available written material, often our inclination is to rely on official reports and known "facts" rather than personal accounts. But most of the pieces presented here are personal memories of Stonewall Jackson, for official reports are written and facts interpreted by the same species that records its experiences, conclusions, and opinions in letters, diaries, and memoirs. Indeed, it is the opinion of (co-editor) David Novak, who has found much contradiction between what he saw and experienced in the field in Vietnam and what he has read about the same events in official reports, that the personal account should be respected.

It is also important to remember that soldiers in the field have more than a passing interest in their commander, for their fate is in his hands. When Stonewall did nothing more remarkable than ride along their line, the men watched him so intensely that even after the passing of the years they could remember what he looked like, what he did, and what he said in the few minutes their eyes were on him. Although the accumulation of detail these old soldiers often employ in their description is sometimes considered exaggeration, it is as likely, I think, to be nothing more than the revealed treasure of a memory made keen and rich by the life-and-death world of war they lived in.

Added to all this is the fact that the hopes of the Confederates' young, struggling, and in many ways (at least arguably) mistaken and misdirected but intensely sincere nation were, in the end, vested in such military leaders as Stonewall Jackson--warrior-chief in life, warrior-saint in death. I record here the following from a lovely South Carolinian, the simple but revealing prayer her grandfather, an old Confederate, said at every meal to the end of his life:

> *P.G.T. Beauregard,*
> *Barnard E. Bee,*
> *Stonewall Jackson,*
> *Robert E. Lee.*
>   Amen

SHORNE HARRISON

ACKNOWLEDGEMENTS

We sincerely thank the following: Megan Fox, of the Library of the Graduate School of Management, Simmons College, Boston, Massachusetts; Lynda E. Wadsworth, artistic consultant; Lisa McCown and Vaughan Stanley of the Special Collections at the Leyburn Library, Washington & Lee University in Lexington, Virginia; the late Kenneth Lueder of Omaha, Nebraska; Diane Jacob of the Virginia Military Institute Archives in Lexington; Keith Gibson and Jeff Jackson of the VMI Museum; the staff of the Jones Memorial Library, Lynchburg, Virginia; Mrs. Walter E. Long, wife of the late Dr. Walter E. Long; the staff of the Maryland Historical Society in Baltimore, Maryland; photographer Mike Collingwood of Lexington; the staff of the Museum of the Confederacy in Richmond, Virginia; the staff of the Maine State Library in Augusta, Maine; Joanna Smith, formerly of the Stonewall Jackson House and now Washington and Lee University, both in Lexington; Warwick Publishing Company, Lynchburg, Virginia; and the staff of Stonewall Jackson's Headquarters at Winchester, Virginia.

SH
DN
MN

NEAR LEXINGTON, VIRGINIA
(Photograph, late 1800's)

". . . I have a lovely view of Mountain scenery. Lexington is the most beautiful place that I remember ever having seen when taken in connexion with the surrounding country."
—THOMAS JONATHAN JACKSON, in a letter to his sister Laura Arnold, August 20, 1851

JACKSON'S BELOVED, LAST HOME: "THE GRANARY OF THE CONFEDERACY"
AS TAKEN FROM
THE OFFICIAL PROGRAM
OF THE 42ND ANNUAL CONFEDERATE REUNION
IN
RICHMOND, VIRGINIA, 1932

The Shenandoah Valley of Virginia was the place where Jackson lived, loved, and, during the Civil War, waged his most famous campaign. It was also the home of many of the men who were in his ranks. At their reunion in 1932 the old Confederates included in their official program a description of the valley that had played such a large part in their lives, in the life of their fallen hero, and in the course of the Civil War.

The rolling country of the Valley of Virginia, flanked by the Blue Ridge on the east and the Alleghenies on the west, drained by the winding Shenandoah, and cut by the picturesque Massanutten range which rises out of the plain near Strasburg and ends abruptly within the northern boundary of Rockingham County, not only attracts visitors because of its scenic panorama of beauty and charm, but will ever arouse the interest of those who find delight in historic deeds of the past. This region played a most significant part in the epoch-making struggle between the North and South, for its unusual fertility and wealth and its geographical form and location made its control of material of strategic importance to the armies of the Confederacy.

The "Granary of the Confederacy" had for many years been famous for the production of wheat and other grains. And it is not surprising that in this valley Cyrus H. McCormick invented and perfected his reaper, which, by strange irony, through its later use on the prairies of the Mid-West, became one of the most effective weapons employed by the North against Virginia and the South, to which Mr. McCormick always felt warmly attached.

While secession was not popular in the Valley at first, sentiment definitely turned after it was evident that Lincoln intended to use force. The governor of Virginia, John Letcher, who was from that section, opposed secession, but he began to favor it when the President called upon him for Virginia's quota of volunteers. Among those who persisted in their loyalty to the Union [was] . . . Reverend George Junkin, father-in-law of Stonewall Jackson and a native of Pennsylvania who had served as an able and popular president of Washington College since 1848.

It was evident from the beginning that Virginia would be the major battleground of the war, and the State's famous Valley, with its mountainous flanks had to be taken into consideration in any offensive or defensive plans of either the North or South.

It should be observed that while the Valley provided the best route for invasion from Virginia into the North, the reverse was not true, for an army following its course southwest would move away from rather than toward Richmond. However, in every campaign for the advance on Richmond the Union commanders had to guard against an attack on Washington by way of the Valley, and this fact enabled General Lee on several important occasions to keep the Northern armies divided over a wide territory.

But the town of the Valley which is the shrine of the South, and which attracts thousands of visitors from all over the country, is not the town in which the greatest battle was fought, but that in which the Commander-in-Chief of the Confederate armies spent the last years of his life endeavoring to teach the young men of the South to be useful citizens of a reunited country. General Lee ennobled the position of college president by serving as the head of Washington College in Lexington from August 1865 till his death on October 12, 1870.

The most cherished traditions of the University of Lexington [*Washington & Lee University*] are associated with the life and personality of Robert Edward Lee. On the campus is the General's home, the Lee Chapel, built under his supervision, which contains the Lee Museum, his office preserved as he left it, and the recumbent statue of Lee by the eminent sculptor, Edward Valentine, late of Richmond. It is the stately simplicity and naturalness conveyed by this statue that impresses the visitor probably more than anything else in Lexington. In the crypt below the statue are the remains of General Lee, his father "Light Horse Harry" Lee, and other members of the family.

The memory of General Stonewall Jackson is inseparably connected with the history of the Virginia Military Institute, where he served as Professor of Military Science and Natural Philosophy from [1851] till the beginning of the war. After his death at Chancellorsville, his body was brought home to Lexington where he is honored today by a large bronze statue in the cemetery. [*His house on East Washington Street--the only home he ever owned--is open to the public.*]

Matthew Fontaine Maury, the "Pathfinder of the Seas," to whom every ocean traveler is indebted, and a man especially honored by every important nation of the earth, supervised the coast defenses of the Confederacy, and after its fall became a member of the cabinet of the Emperor Maximilian in Mexico. He later returned to Lexington and served as a professor at the Virginia Military Institute for five years until his death. A monument to his memory has been erected in the beautiful Goshen Pass, near Lexington, which he made forever famous by his dying request that

JACKSON'S HOME IN THE VALLEY
Thomas and Mary Anna Jackson's house at 8 East Washington Street, ca. 1860, Lexington, Virginia

his body be borne through it when the laurels were in bloom.

The rapid movements and brilliant strategy in General Jackson's famous Valley Campaign in the spring of 1862 will always interest the general reader as well as the student of military science. The Campaign, so ably executed by Jackson, should be remembered as a part of Lee's masterful plan for the defense of Richmond. As a part of his plan Lee ordered a vigorous offensive in the Valley to serve as a strategic diversion of the Federal troops to prevent the junction of the several Union armies under Banks, Fremont, McDowell, and McClellan. No abler man than General Jackson could have been chosen to execute such orders. After an earlier repulse at Kernstown, in May 1862 Jackson moved forward vigorously and, by his rapid movements and skillfully planned attacks, entirely mystified the enemy and ultimately put them to flight, enabling himself to escape and go to the aid of Lee in defense of Richmond. Within a month he had marched 400 miles, fought six pitched battles, the most important of which was at Winchester on May 25, and captured thousands of prisoners and valuable supplies. In addition, he had not only prevented the union of the Federal armies but

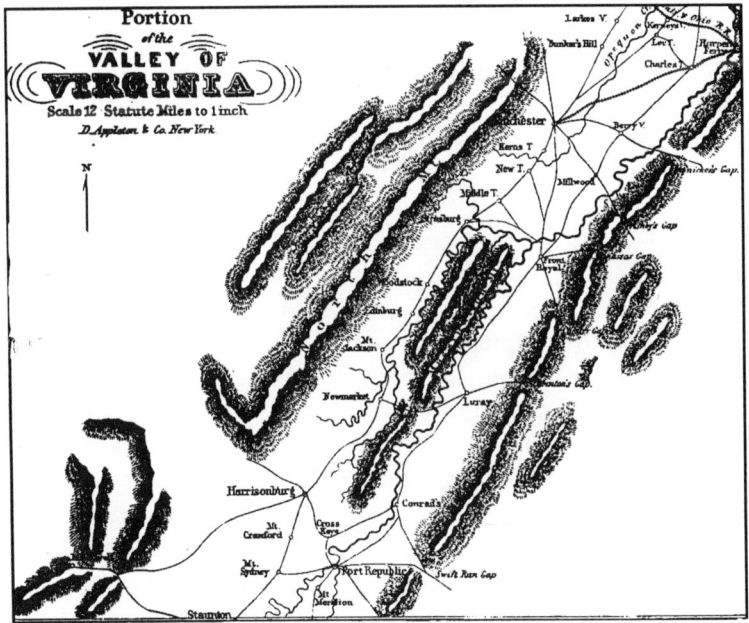

SHENANDOAH VALLEY

This map shows the part of the Shenandoah Valley where Jackson operated during the Civil War. Not shown is his beloved Lexington which is a little more than 30 miles south of Staunton (the southernmost town shown on this map).

also had terrified the Federal officials who made rapid plans for the defense of Washington which they thought was in immediate danger.

With the shifting of the scene of battle from Union territory to Virginia in 1864, the Valley was the scene of new combats. It was on May 15, 1864, that the "Charge of the Cadets" from the Virginia Military Institute was made at New Market. While this charge had little effect on the outcome of the war, it will long be remembered because of the courageous heroism of the boys whose action is commemorated in an impressive ceremony held by their alma mater each year. Major Theodore S. Long, of the Federal Commander's staff, wrote: "I must say that I have never witnessed a more gallant advance and final charge than was given by those brave boys on that field. They fought like veterans."

In June, Federal troops under General Hunter made a raid southward. At Lexington, Governor Letcher's home and the buildings of the Virginia Military Institute were burned and the buildings of Washington College pillaged and damaged. In the same raid the Houdon statue of Washington was taken from the campus of the Institute, but was restored after the war. Colonel Hayes and Major McKinley, of Hunter's command on this occasion, were afterwards Presidents of the United States. Hunter was forced westward by General Early, who now cleared the Valley of Federal troops and appeared at the very gates of Washington.

Meanwhile General Sheridan was ordered to the Valley, which he proceeded to make void of nearly everything which could be of immediate use to man or beast so that, according to his own boast, even a crow in flying over the country "would have to carry his own rations." No portion of the Valley became better known than the region around Winchester, a town of important historical connections for nearly two hundred years, and where still are to be seen the houses used as headquarters by Generals Washington, Jackson, and Sheridan. It is said that during the war this town changed hands between North and South seventy-two times, four times on one day. Through the entire length of the Valley Pike are to be found markers and monuments reminding the traveler of significant battles and events, most of which are connected with the "War between the States." ♦

COURTESY WINCHESTER-FREDERICK COUNTY
HISTORICAL SOCIETY ARCHIVES
STONEWALL JACKSON'S HEADQUARTERS
November 1861-March 1862, Winchester, Virginia

ALLEN CHRISTIAN REDWOOD
A photograph taken during the war

ALLEN CHRISTIAN REDWOOD
BY
SHORNE HARRISON

The memories of Stonewall Jackson which comprise this book are primarily those of men who served under him in the Confederate Army--in his brigade or division or corps; these men include the articulate and the near-illiterate; they rank from private to general. They speak of the man and the battles, of the waiting in camp and the exhausting marches, of the great victories and the terrible losses. And they appear in their own words. There is the determined and rugged young rebel Andrew Davidson Long; the once recalcitrant but later gallantly obedient James A. Walker; the young Ted Barclay, facing immortality in mortal combat.

The kind, efficient Dr. Hunter Holmes McGuire has much to say about his friend and commander, and John Newton Lyle, who observed Jackson on the streets of Lexington, in bivouac and on the battlefield, speaks again and again on these pages about what he saw. But of the men who appear in this collection, the most fully represented is the artist-writer Allen Christian Redwood. Redwood is little known today, but he deserves attention, especially as regards his treatment, as both writer and artist, of his favorite subject(s): Stonewall Jackson and his men. Much of the writing and many of the illustrations in this volume are from his pen.

Redwood was born on June 19, 1844, at the home of his maternal grandparents, a plantation called "Prospect Hill" in Lancaster County, Virginia. His family soon moved to Baltimore, where he was educated in private academies, and in 1860 Redwood moved to New York City with his father, where he attended the Brooklyn Poly-

A. C. REDWOOD

BEHIND THE STONE WALL

This picture, typical of Redwood's work, depicts Cobb's and Kershaw's troops in the sunken road during the first battle of Fredericksburg. Redwood did this illustration for an article by General Longstreet about the Battle of Fredericksburg which appeared in *Battles and Leaders, Volume 3*, 1888.

technic Institute until the Civil War began in April 1861. Soon after, he returned to Virginia and--only weeks after his seventeenth birthday--enlisted as a private in the Middlesex Southrons, which eventually formed part of the 55th Virginia Infantry, Field's Brigade, A. P. Hill's Division, Stonewall Jackson's Corps. He was wounded in action three times and taken prisoner twice. In January 1864, after the death of his beloved Stonewall following the Battle of Chancellorsville in May 1863 and the death of a favorite soldier-friend after the Battle of Gettysburg the following July, Redwood transferred to Company C of the First Maryland Cavalry.

Even as a very young boy Redwood was interested in painting and drawing. Some of his early works still exist, and they reveal a serious and fair talent. During the war the young soldier often sketched camp and battle scenes, but he was not to begin his life's work--the writing about and illustration of the Civil War for the general public--until the 1880's. From 1868 to 1879 he worked in Baltimore as a lithographer at A. Hoen & Co.

A. C. REDWOOD
SELF PORTRAIT
Part of a picture that includes this small self portrait of Redwood holding a snake.

It was after this that he began to submit drawings and articles whose theme was the Civil War to *Scribner's Monthly* (later called *The Century Magazine*), to *Battles and Leaders of the Civil War*, and to the Harper's Publishing Company. His pictures present vivid and "concrete" detail, and his writing is replete with precise color. To recreate long-ago

A. C. REDWOOD

CONFEDERATE ARTILLERY FIRING ON UNION COLUMNS

In this picture, Redwood depicts the Washington Artillery on Marye's Heights, during the Battle of Fredericksburg (December 13, 1862), firing on Union troops forming for an attack. The picture was done for an article in *Battle and Leaders, Volume 3, 1888*, written by First Lieutenant William Miller Owen, CSA.

scenes of war he used his old sketches, new sketches he made upon revisiting the old battlegrounds after the war, and descriptions which he solicited from other old soldiers. But above all he relied on his own memory as an on-scene witness, and fortunately for us it was a memory aided by the eye of the painter and the writer for the details that make art true. General Bradley T. Johnson wrote to Redwood in 1910: "You are the last drawer of the Confederate Soldier who has seen . . . the gaunt, lean, ragged, barefoot Infantry. . . ."

Redwood moved to the New York area to be closer to his publishers, and he worked there some twenty-five years. He never married. When he "retired," he returned once again to Virginia, where he lived with his cousins on the banks of the Rappahannock River, at "Milbanke" (near Port Conway), and continued writing about and painting scenes of the Civil War. His life's work was an obsession born of his need to tell--using all the powers and resources he had--his story of the war, and to memorialize the men who had fought in it alongside him. He once wrote:

A. C. REDWOOD
SAYING GOODBYE
Redwood, wounded in the arm at Gettysburg, saying goodbye to his mortally wounded friend Jack.

xxxi

BARKSDALE'S MISSISSIPPIANS
Battle of Fredericksburg, December 13, 1862

> In the years that have ensued, I . . . have had time to change from boyish trooper . . . to grizzled veteran of sixty-odd, but my memory of those brave days holds out, & the people who made them so are more real [to me] than those of today.

Allen Redwood died December 24, 1922, in Asheville, North Carolina, where he had gone to visit his brother Henry. He is buried in that city, in Henry's family plot at Riverside Cemetery. Writers William Sydney Porter (who went by the name O. Henry) and Thomas Wolfe are also buried at Riverside, and signs point the way to their graves; however, though well known at the turn of the century Allen Redwood is now quite undeservedly almost forgotten--and there is no sign to his resting place.

But his real and lasting legacy, his illustrations, can be seen still today--even in recently published Civil War books and magazines. Sadly, Redwood is seldom recognized as the artist, credit (when it is offered at all) often mistakenly given instead to the engraver.

Unfortunately, it is difficult to determine how true the engravings are to Redwood's originals, as his paintings are not easily available for viewing. But even in the secondhand and somewhat static engravings we can see the telling details of the participant. We can know what Redwood saw and sense some of what he and his comrades felt so very long ago in those days so crucial to their lives and to the life of the nation. For that alone his work must be judged priceless, and his name remembered. ♦

ON TO SHARPSBURG

Here Redwood depicts a portion of Stonewall's Corps crossing the Potomac at White's Ford while on the way into Maryland and the Battle of Sharpsburg (Antietam), September 17, 1862.

PREFACE
BY
James Alexander Walker
CAPTAIN, PULASKI GUARDS
FOURTH VIRGINIA REGIMENT
STONEWALL BRIGADE

James Walker was in the senior class (first class) at the Virginia Military Institute during Jackson's first year as a professor there. Jackson was a dedicated but struggling teacher; Walker was a bright, hotheaded young man who gave Jackson much grief in the classroom. After one particularly heated incident, Jackson put Walker under arrest; as a result the cadet was later court-martialed and dismissed from the Institute without his diploma. He was angry and bitterly disappointed, but went on to become a lawyer, to marry, and to raise a family. Ten years after his dismissal from VMI, Walker found himself in the Stonewall Brigade, where his old professor and now commander took note of his gallantry in action and promoted him. Walker rose in the ranks from captain to brigadier general; he was, in fact, the last commander of the Stonewall Brigade, leading it from Chancellorsville in May 1863 until it was virtually destroyed at the Bloody Angle in May 1864. The contemptuous cadet matured into an admiring subordinate of Mighty Stonewall. The following is from a speech Walker gave at Richmond, Virginia, in 1891.

And why shall not the South have its heroes? . . . The South has its history; its traditions; its wrongs; its ruins; its victories; its defeats; its record of suffering and humiliation; its destruction, and, worse still, its reconstruction. She has many cemeteries filled with her own patriotic dead, slain fighting her battles; and she has on her soil, beneath her bright skies . . . cemeteries, filled with brave men, slain in battle by the hands of her warriors.

. . . For four years the Confederate government floated its flag over every State beneath the Southern cross, and the Confederate armies carried their battle-flag in triumph from the Rio Grande almost to the capital of the Keystone State, and spread terror to the Great Lakes. Its little navy showed the strange colors of the new-born nation from the Northern sea to the equator, driving the American merchant marine from the high seas, until scarcely a ship engaged in commerce dared show the Stars and Stripes on the Atlantic ocean.

For four bloody years the Confederacy stood the shock of all the power and resources of the greatest republic on the face of the globe, and fought for independence on more than one hundred battlefields, and at last, when her armies were worn away by attrition and her means of resistance exhausted, succumbed to "overwhelming numbers and resources."

. . . Was there no heroism in all this? Heroes are not made to order. Deeds make heroes--imperishable deeds, born of virtue, courage, and patriotism. Genius may make men great; power and place may make men famous, but the crown which decks the brow of the true hero is more than genius can give or power and place can bestow.

. . . Jackson's fame is as bright as sun at the noonday; as fixed and imperishable as the everlasting mountain peaks of his native State. When his spirit passed over the river and rested under the shade of the trees, the unspotted soul of a Christian hero went to its reward. . . . Amid the lurid lightnings, fierce passions, and dead thunders of the greatest civil war of modern times, when men's minds were full of evil machinations, and their hearts filled with hatred, malice, and all uncharitableness, he laid down his life; and yet, strange to tell, not one word of unkindness or reproach assailed his memory. The most implacable of our foes breathed no word of criticism or charged him with a single act or speech unbecoming a true Christian hero. If Stonewall Jackson was not a hero, then the history of the world, its wars and revolutions, its struggles for country and freedom, never knew a man worthy to wear that title.

◆

STONEWALL

Although opinions vary as to exactly when this photograph was taken, it is generally agreed that it was made in the fall of 1862. While in Winchester, Virginia, Stonewall was persuaded to go to the Routzahn Gallery on Loudoun Street to sit for his portrait. This and the photograph from which the *carte de visite* on the front cover was made are the only known photographs of Jackson taken during the Civil War.

PROFESSOR MAJOR T. J. JACKSON, 1855
"He passed in the community as a sensible, odd man, of undoubted courage, energy and goodness. He was a man whom it was no easy matter to know."

– *JOHN NEWTON LYLE*

PART I

TEACHER, HUSBAND, SOLDIER

THOMAS JONATHAN JACKSON,
First Lieutenant of Artillery
This ambrotype was most likely taken in late August of 1847, toward the end of the Mexican War.

THOMAS JONATHAN JACKSON
BY
SHORNE HARRISON

The man we know as Stonewall Jackson was born January 21, 1824, in Clarksburg, Virginia (now West Virginia), and until he was 37 years old lived his life as Thomas Jonathan Jackson. When he was only two, his older sister Elizabeth and his lawyer father Jonathan died of typhoid. His mother remarried and soon after, Tom, his older brother Warren, and his younger sister Laura were sent to live with relatives. Young Tom Jackson was raised at Jackson's Mill, the (West) Virginia farm of his bachelor uncle, Cummins Jackson, a rather untamed man whose home nevertheless provided the young boy a much needed sense of security and a source of affection, especially after the death of his mother when he was seven.

Poorly educated in the backwoods of western Virginia, Jackson was determined to gain the free college education which West Point offered. Some luck and a great deal of perseverance helped him win an appointment to the school, and hard work and his ever-present, fierce persistence advanced him from the bottom of the class to 17th in a class of 59 by the time he graduated in June 1846. (General McClellan was second in this class).

After graduation, Jackson--like so many other young military officers of the day--applied his practical military training in the Mexican War. Second Lieutenant Thomas Jonathan Jackson proved capable enough under fire at Contreras, Churabusco, and Chapultepec to be brevetted for bravery (three times within six months), and in 1848 he left Mexico a major.

The life in garrison which followed did not suit Jackson as well as the field of battle, and in 1851 he took a

JACKSON AT TWENTY-FOUR YEARS

position as professor of natural philosophy (physics and astronomy) and artillery tactics at the Virginia Military Institute ("the West Point of the South") in the beautiful Shenandoah Valley town of Lexington, resigning in early 1852 from the regular army.

Though a decidedly uninspired teacher who lacked not only talent but also imagination and tact in the classroom, and a man who was stiff and rather eccentric in society, Major Jackson proved to be an interested and active member of the community and an unusually loving husband to both his wives.

He fell in love with Elinor Junkin and married her in 1853. She was the daughter of the President of Washington College (now Washington and Lee University), and it was with the Junkins in their house on campus that "Ellie" and Thomas Jackson made their home for the next 14 months, until Ellie died from complications of childbirth, preceded by her stillborn baby boy. Jackson was broken hearted and inconsolable.

For months he struggled to accept the loss of his young wife. A trip to Europe which he took in 1856 seems to have healed his sorrow enough to allow him to love again; in 1857 he married Mary Anna Morrison (called "Anna"), the daughter of the President of Davidson College (located in Salem, North Carolina). Like Ellie's, Anna's first child (a daughter named Mary Graham) did not live, and though Jackson loved children and longed for a family (a daughter, Julia, who lived to young adulthood was not born until after the war had begun), Anna and he shared a happy home nevertheless. An observer of the couple in Lexington noted that

> [t]o have seen [Anna and Major Jackson] walking the streets you would have thought him a lover, trying to win her affection. He did not cram his hands into his pockets and go strolling ahead,

MAJOR THOMAS J. JACKSON

ELINOR JUNKIN JACKSON

whistling a tune after the true married man's style, leaving the madam to make her way after him the best she could. He was all attention as he walked at her side, handing her tenderly over crossings and showing her all those delicate attentions that lovers practice and husbands forget before the honeymoon has reached its second quarter.

Jackson was serious and dutiful about his teaching obligations at the Institute, and involved in business, cultural, and, especially, religious aspects of life in Lexington. In fact, that facet of Jackson's life which entered into every other part of it was his devotion to God.

For ten years, Major Thomas Jackson--husband, professor, and active member of the community--lived a comfortable and peaceful life in Lexington. But by the end of his decade in that quiet Valley village, rumors of war were being heard everywhere in the land, and on April 12, 1861, when Confederate guns fired on Fort Sumter, the Civil War began. On Sunday, April 21, 1861, Major Jackson was summoned from his pleasant, brick home on Washington Street to that war. And in it he was to engrave his name not only on its battlefields but, also--as the present volume shows--in the hearts of the men who served in his ranks. This in spite of his forced marches and his hard discipline, for, as one of the surgeons with his brigade noted, "[h]e . . . outlived every prejudice," and by the time of his death was "regarded [as] a great Military Chieftain. . . ."

In short, to most of the men who were his troops Stonewall Jackson was, as one of them observed, "greatest and noblest in that he was good, and . . . gave his talent and his life to a cause that, as before the God he so devoutly served, he deemed right and just." ♦

COURTESY STONEWALL JACKSON HOUSE

MARY ANNA JACKSON

"As it takes a combination of the male and female to make up a complete man, so it took T. J. and Anna Jackson together to shape up such a character as Stonewall Jackson."

– *JOHN NEWTON LYLE*

COURTESY SHORNE HARRISON
GENERAL THOMAS JONATHAN JACKSON

LEXINGTON, VIRGINIA

A photograph taken by Michael Miley (1890's) from the corner of Main and Washington Streets, looking south down Main Street.

COURTESY SPECIAL COLLECTIONS, LEYBURN LIBRARY, WASHINGTON & LEE UNIVERSITY

JACKSON IN LEXINGTON
BY
JOHN NEWTON LYLE
FIRST LIEUTENANT, COMPANY I
LIBERTY HALL VOLUNTEERS
FOURTH VIRGINIA REGIMENT
STONEWALL BRIGADE

John Lyle was born July 29, 1839, in Botetourt County, Virginia. He graduated from Washington College (now Washington and Lee University) in Lexington, Virginia, in 1861 and in June of the same year enlisted in the Liberty Hall Volunteers, a company of boys from Washington College who served in the Stonewall Brigade. He was captured in March 1862 and exchanged in August of that year, after which he enlisted in the 19th Virginia Cavalry. After the war Lyle was a lawyer and a judge in Virginia and an editor in Texas. In later life he recorded his wartime memoirs, "Stonewall Jackson's Guard," which exist today in typescript in the Special Collections of the Leyburn Library, Washington and Lee University, Lexington, Virginia.

During his college days, just prior to the Civil War, Lyle frequently saw Major Jackson on the streets of Lexington; here he describes the experience of actually meeting the professor.

He lived in the village of Lexington and walked to and from the Institute every day. I roomed whilst at Washington College--from 1858-1861--in the front room in the second story of [M]ain [B]uilding on the right of the hall as you face East, and had day board at Mr. Compton's, who lived opposite the Episcopal church. The road to the Institute, at that time, passed West of the church, and East of the College, bisecting the present campus about where the Lee Memorial Chapel now stands. On the way to breakfast, I met Major Jackson nearly every day, striding along in his rolling gait with his chin stuck out and the beak of his cap well down over his eyes. He made indeed a solemn precession that I would no more have thought of interrupting than I would have dared poke up a sleeping tiger. It filled the youthful breast with awe. Its awfulness as I afterwards learned was only in appearance....

In the spring of 1861, when war excitement was running high, a rumor reached college that our neighbors, the cadets of the Virginia Military Institute, had been ordered to the field. We were all on our heads to get the facts. Meeting Major Jackson one morning in front of the church, my eagerness for reliable news getting the better of my awe for the man, I made bold to stop and interview him. The moment I accosted him, his "shell" dropped off, a pleasant smile overspread his face, and to my questions came replies in pleasant[,] winning tones. If I had seen the cloud-wrapped Jupiter smile from high Olympus, I could not have been more astonished. I fell dead in love then and there with the "inside" Jackson, though my awe of him with shell on never left me. ♦

STONEWALL JACKSON'S SCABBARD SPEECH
BY
WILLIAM ALEXANDER OBENCHAIN
CADET DRILLMASTER, VMI, CLASS OF 1862
LATER MAJOR, FIELD'S DIVISION
LONGSTREET'S CORPS

William A. Obenchain was born April 27, 1841, in Buchanan, Virginia, and graduated first in his class "with distinction" from VMI in the class of 1862, which like the 1862 class at West Point actually received their diplomas in 1861. He went to Richmond the same year (1861) with the corps of cadets and then served as a lieutenant in the Confederate army until he was promoted to captain for "skill and meritorious conduct." In 1864 he became, on General Lee's orders, an engineer in Field's Division, Longstreet's Corps. After the war he was a professor at and later, for 27 years, president of Ogden College in Bowling Green, Kentucky. He died August 17, 1916.

The incident Obenchain describes below took place in Lexington, Virginia, in April 1861--before Lincoln's threatened use of force against the South had turned the citizens of Lexington against the Union. While the young, high-spirited cadets at the Virginia Military Institute were very early on secessionists and all for the "revolution," the majority of the townspeople still hoped to preserve the Union. One of the results of this difference of opinion between the cadets and the people of Lexington was a confrontation between the two groups which Edward A. Moore--who was a cannoneer in Jackson's command in the Civil War--described as follows:

> *One afternoon, while a huge Union flag-pole was being raised on the street, when half-way up snapped and fell to the ground in pieces, I witnessed a personal encounter between a cadet and a [pro-Union man] . . . which was promptly taken up by their friends. The cadets who were present hastened to their barracks and, joined by their comrades, armed themselves, and with fixed bayonets came streaming at the double-quick toward town. They were met at the end of Main [S]treet by their professors. . . . After considerable persuasion the cadets were induced to return to their barracks.*

After returning to the barracks the cadets were

COURTESY VIRGINIA MILITARY INSTITUTE ARCHIVES
VIRGINIA MILITARY INSTITUTE
Lexington, Virginia, 1857

Looking northeast toward the Blue Ridge, this view of VMI shows it as it was when Major Thomas Jonathan Jackson taught there.

assembled in Major Preston's section-room, which had the largest seating capacity in the building. The object of the meeting was the pacification of the cadets and the prevention of further trouble. To this end speeches were made by the superintendent and others, and then a long pause ensued. Amongst the academic officers present was one who was conspicuous by the bolt-upright position in which he sat. His body did not touch the back of his chair, and his large hands rested motionless on his thighs. Usually he kept his eyes to the front, but on this occasion he was closely scanning the faces and reading the thoughts of the young men before him. This person was no other than Major Thomas Jonathan Jackson. In church he always sat in the same posture, never touching the back of the pew nor turning his eyes from the preacher. If during a dull sermon he ever fell asleep (and he had been seen to close his eyes at times) he always retained this position. It is no wonder that he afterwards received--with baptism of fire-- the immortal name of "Stonewall."

Major Jackson then seemed most eminent for Christian piety, a stern, unwavering sense of duty, a noble straightforwardness, and a beautiful simplicity of nature. In short, he exhibited that strong individuality which always accompanies genius, but which the world's stupidity characterizes only as eccentricity. . . . His singularity was often ridiculed, and his peculiar ways were a subject of mimicry. Although possessing such manly virtues, he was regarded by cadets and others as "a failure" as a teacher. He was wanting in tact in the classroom, although he afterwards displayed such brilliant tactics on the field. In his classes he never asked leading questions.

If the student was not familiar with the subject, and requested a repetition of the question, with the hope of a change of words embodying a useful hint, he was sure to get it again in the identical words, and even with the same emphasis and peculiar intonation of voice. By some this was considered indicative of lack of thoroughness in the subjects he professed to teach. But the fact is, Jackson had but one way of saying things, and the best matured and most direct. He was clumsy, and often unsatisfactory in his experiments [in the classroom]. All this, together with his eccentricity, caused him to be looked upon as an unpractical man.

He was also unpopular as the butt of the school. At times, on his way to and from barracks, walking as usual with measured step, body erect and eyes to the front, cadets have been known to throw stones just in front of him, not to strike him, but on a wager that he could not be made to look around. On he would go, without ever turning his head or changing his gait, or, as some have alleged, without even blinking his eyes. Up to the time the writer became a second-class man, when, by the voluntary action of his--the leading--section, such conduct was broken up, it had been the custom of the members of Jackson's classes to create wanton disorder in his section-room, often to the extent of downright disrespect. He was imperturbable throughout it all, never losing his dignity. . . .

But if held by many in low estimate as a teacher of Physics and Astronomy, he was respected by all for the gallantry he had displayed in the Mexican War. His military record was well known, and criticism of his methods in the classroom was frequently off-set by some remark as, "But old Jack knows how to fight." His conscientious discharge of duty and uniform soldierly bearing could not but be admired. As an instructor in artillery tactics he gave satisfaction. His explanations of the battery movements were clear and concise, and his commands were given with determination and force. He alone of all the officers of the Institute pronounced the word "oblique" in his commands as if spelled *oblike*. Another peculiarity was the manner in which he carried his sabre when walking to or from duty. Although belted around him, he invariably held it in a horizontal position, well up under his left arm, handle to the rear, curved edge up, and left hand seizing the scabbard near the middle.

Now that civil war was daily becoming more probable, and the strain of excitement was too great for much interest in academic studies, Major Jackson began to be estimated less by his qualifications for the classroom than by his fitness for the field.

. . . That Jackson possessed courage, no one doubted; that he was well suited for subordinate command, and, if so ordered, would march unflinchingly into the jaws of death, everyone believed; but if asked to name the professor at the Institute most likely to rise to the highest rank and win the greatest fame in the event of war, probably four cadets out of five would have thought Jackson last.

As mentioned above, after several speeches had been made there ensued a long pause. Perhaps some reply was expected from the cadets. At last the painful silence was broken by a cadet crying out, "Major Jackson!" The cry was taken up by others, until it became general and continuous. Aware of Jackson's awkwardness and shyness, many may have called for him in the spirit of mischief; but doubtless the majority of the cadets, knowing his straightforwardness and sense of justice, desired from him some expression of approval and sympathy. Rising from his seat, he was greeted with loud applause. He waited until the noise had subsided; then, with body erect and eyes sparkling, as they did so often afterwards on the field of battle, he said, with vigor and fluency that were a surprise to all:

A SECTION ROOM AT VMI

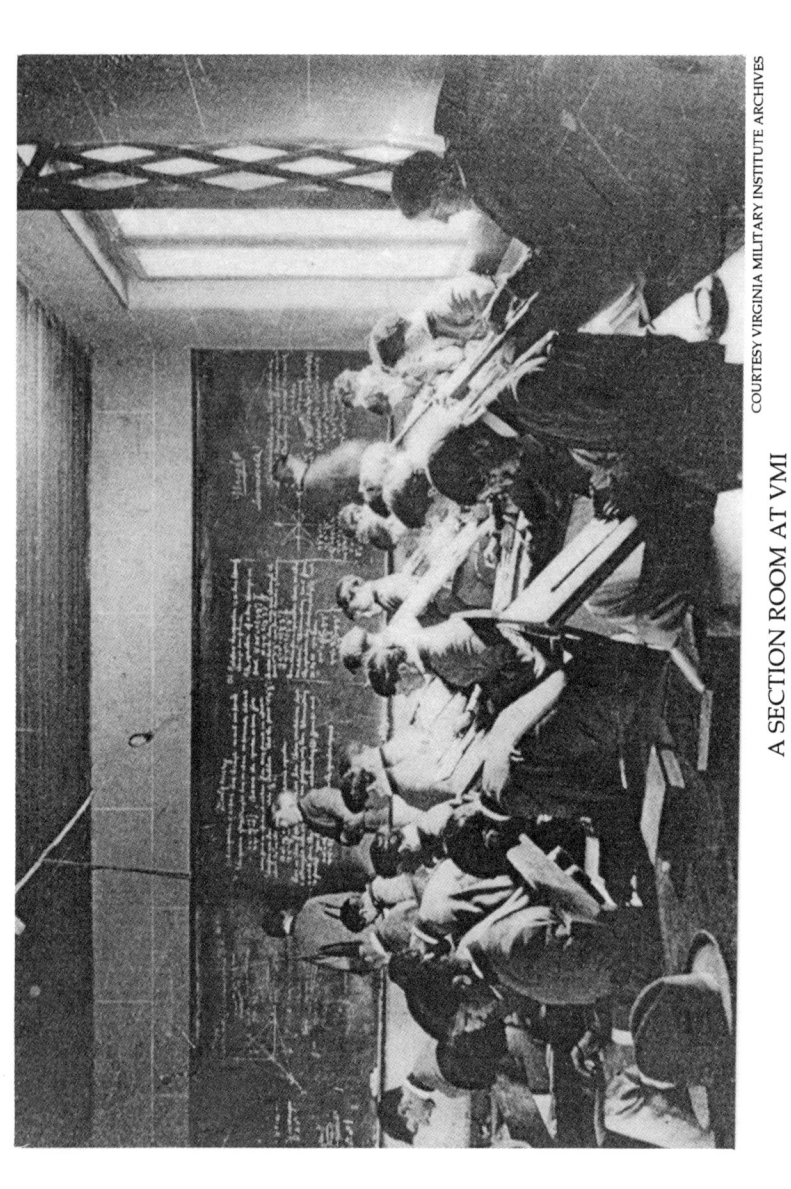

Taken by Michael Miley (whose hat is at lower left) some twenty years after Jackson taught at VMI, this photograph of a typical classroom at the Institute shows little change from Jackson's time.

COURTESY VIRGINIA MILITARY INSTITUTE ARCHIVES

Military men, when they make speeches, should say but a few words, and speak them to the point. I admire, young gentlemen, the spirit you have shown in rushing to the defen[s]e of your comrades; but I must commend you particularly for the readiness with which you have listened to the counsel and obeyed the orders of your superior officer. The time may be near at hand when your State will need your services, and if that time does come, then draw your swords and throw away the scabbards.

Pregnant events followed in rapid succession. News was not received until the next day of the bombardment and surrender of Fort Sumter. There was no telegraph line to Lexington in those days. On Monday [April 15, 1861] news came of Lincoln's proclamation calling for seventy-five thousand men. On the following Wednesday Virginia seceded from the Union. The Rockbridge Rifles had already received marching orders. Excitement was now intense. After the secession of the State, public sentiment was entirely revolutionized. But one feeling filled every breast--loyalty to the State and resistance to coercion. Before setting out on their march down the Valley, the Rockbridge Rifles came to the arsenal [at VMI] to complete their equipment for active service. Volunteers and cadets mingled freely on the grounds, extending hands in friendship and swearing to die together for the Old Dominion. Some of the Rifles said to a group of cadets, "Boys, you were right." Only a few days before they were ready to shoot each other down in the streets. How quickly a common cause obliterates individual differences.

On the following Sunday, the 21st of April, the corps of cadets, under the command of Major Jackson, was on its way to Richmond. ♦

COURTESY VIRGINIA MILITARY INSTITUTE ARCHIVES
DRILLMASTERS FOR JACKSON
These five cadets from VMI were with Major Jackson at Richmond in 1861. Here they wear their "furlough uniforms."

"Their first post of duty was Camp Lee. After rendering that place and the Baptist Church excellent and much needed service as drill officers of infantry, they scattered in the field, where all served their cause well, not a few with distinction, and many to find a soldier's grave."

– HUNTER HOLMES McGUIRE

ON THE WAY TO WAR
BY
GEORGE HENRY MOFFETT
SERGEANT, COMPANY F
11TH VIRGINIA CAVALRY
AND
JOHN NEWTON LYLE

Both George Henry Moffett (sometimes spelled "Moffatt") and John Newton Lyle were students at Washington College when the Civil War began and witnessed much that went on at the College and in Lexington during those tumultuous days. Eventually, they both became members of the Liberty Hall Volunteers.

George Moffett was born March 3, 1845, in Huntersville, Pocahantas County, Virginia (later West Virginia), and at the age of 18 the tall, brown-haired youth had already graduated from college and was on his way to war with the LHV as a private in Company I. He was later transferred to the 11th Cavalry and promoted to sergeant and then, in 1863, to sergeant major. He was captured at Greenbriar River near Hillsboro, Pocahantas County, December 21, 1863--perhaps taking risks near his home at Christmas. He was sent to Wheeling, then to Camp Chase (January 1, 1864). On March 14, 1864, he was sent to Fort Delaware where he was confined until several months after the war when he finally "took the oath."

After the war Moffett was variously a farmer, a teacher, a lawyer, and member and speaker of the West Virginia House of Delegates. But it was in the newspaper business that he spent most of his later years. He was editor of THE WHEELING REGISTER *until 1884 when he moved to and worked for newspapers in St. Paul, Minnesota, and Portland, Oregon (where he owned* THE EVENING TELEGRAPH*), and Washington, D.C. (where he was the "travelling correspondent" for the* CINCINNATI ENQUIRER*). He died in Washington August 29, 1912.*

When, in April, 1861, news reached Lexington that the Ordinance of Secession had been passed, the sleepy old town [which had been divided in opinion about a war, but quickly aligned itself with the "rebellion"] seemed suddenly changed to a military camp, and on every side were seen the preparations for war. It was decided that the eldest cadets at the military institute should be sent to the various recruiting stations to drill the volunteers, and so one fine day [April 21, 1861], with Jackson at their head, they marched away. The time for their departure was a still, sunny Sunday morning, and all the people of the town gathered to see them off.

The cadets, numbering 200 [*the actual number was between 175-200*], were drawn up in front of the fortress-like building [*the main building at VMI*], waiting for Jackson's appearance. After a time he came . . . out through the gateway. . . . He had barely reached the head of the column, and, wheeling, stood facing the crowd, when, taking off his hat, he said in a low voice: "Let us pray"; and then an aged minister of the town, Dr. White [*from the Presbyterian Church*] raised his voice in prayer. When he had finished, Jackson [waited until the campus clock struck "high noon," then] faced his men: "Forward, march!" and obeying his command, they marched away.

--George Henry Moffett

◆

Once outside Lexington, the cadets--who had marched this far in columns-- boarded stagecoaches and other horse-drawn vehicles for the trip to the train depot in Staunton.

The cadet battalion from the Institute under command of Major T.J. Jackson . . . passed over [the road from Fairfield to Staunton], enroute to Richmond. . . . . . . [T]hey were transported in stage coaches from Lexington to Staunton. A few miles from the latter town, the front coach in the line broke down and brought the column to a halt. When "Old Jack," who was on horseback, and some distance in the rear, hastened forward to ascertain what had checked the progress of his troops, he found the dismounted cadets in high glee and cutting up monkeyshines over their disabled conveyance. Taking a glance at the situation, he ordered the rear to the front, resumed the march, directing the youngsters to repair their vehicle and report to him on their reaching camp. They had to foot it into town and rejoined their comrades late that night, footsore and weary. The breakdown had ceased to be funny.

--JOHN NEWTON LYLE

From Staunton the cadets took the train to Richmond and from Richmond they were sent to various stations to help drill the thousands of volunteers now streaming in. Jackson, after receiving a new commission as a colonel of Virginia volunteers on April 27, 1861, was sent to Harper's Ferry where he assumed command on April 29.

JACKSON'S OLD CAP
Jackson wore this old gray cap (his favorite) through many a campaign in 1861 and 1862. When it was "no longer fit to wear" he reluctantly gave it to his map maker, Jed Hotchkiss.

THOMAS J. JACKSON
The above 1851 portrait was most likely taken by the famous Civil War photographer Matthew Brady in New York City. The insignia have been painted onto the original negative plate.

PART II

THE WAR BEGINS

COURTESY SPECIAL COLLECTIONS, LEYBURN LIBRARY,
WASHINGTON & LEE UNIVERSITY

GOODBYE TO WASHINGTON COLLEGE

A Michael Miley photograph (1890's) of Lexington showing what is now Washington & Lee University in the background. In the spring of 1861 students on the way to war looked up at what was then Washington College—some for the last time—and one student-soldier remembered his thoughts as they left town:

> "Our route [to Harper's Ferry] was down the Valley Turnpike—the old plank road—which took us past the front of the college, a few hundred yards to the left. I looked it a loving farewell. It had been my home for three happy years, and I favored its very dust.
>
> "... I can see it now, its tall white columns gleaming in the sunshine of that bright June morning."

— JOHN NEWTON LYLE

GENERAL THOMAS J. JACKSON
BY
DR. HUNTER HOLMES MCGUIRE
AT FIRST A PRIVATE IN COMPANY F
SECOND VIRGINIA INFANTRY
STONEWALL BRIGADE
AND LATER CHIEF SURGEON OF THE SECOND CORPS
OF THE ARMY OF NORTHERN VIRGINIA

Hunter Holmes McGuire was from Winchester, Virginia. He graduated from medical school at the age of 20, after which--at the age of 22--he taught medicine in Philadelphia. At the beginning of the Civil War, he enlisted in the Second Virginia Infantry Regiment as a private. Soon, however, he joined Jackson's command as chief surgeon. After General Jackson's death McGuire became the medical director of Lee's army, and after the war he joined the faculty of the Virginia Medical College.

These memories of Stonewall Jackson are selected from an article featuring Dr. McGuire which first appeared in the July 19, 1891, issue of the RICHMOND DISPATCH, *just before the July 21st unveiling of the bronze statue of Jackson by Edward Valentine at Lexington, Virginia. The complete article was subsequently reprinted in the* SOUTHERN HISTORICAL SOCIETY PAPERS, *the source of these selections. Dr. McGuire became a close and steady friend to Jackson and remained so until the day Stonewall died.*

I went to Harper's Ferry [in the spring of 1861] . . . as a member of Company F, Second Virginia Regiment, and soon after, for the first time in my life, I saw Jackson. At that time he was a colonel. He was then commanding the army at Harper's Ferry, which was known as the Army of the Shenandoah. Soon after reaching Harper's Ferry I was commissioned by Governor Letcher, who then commanded the Virginia forces, as medical director of that army. When I reported to General Jackson for duty he looked at me a long time without speaking a word, and presently said: "You can go back to your quarters and wait there until you hear from me."

I went back to my quarters and didn't hear a word

COURTESY SHORNE HARRISON
DR. HUNTER McGUIRE
This charcoal drawing of Dr. McGuire was made from a photograph taken of him in later life.

from him for a week, when one evening I was announced at dress-parade as medical director of the army.

Some months afterwards, when I asked the General the cause of the delay, he said that I looked so young that he had sent to Richmond to see if there wasn't some mistake.

Not long after this General Joe Johnston succeeded Colonel Jackson in command of the army, and the latter was given command of all the Virginia forces at Harper's Ferry. Shortly after General Johnston took command I was relieved from duty by some regular old army surgeon. Jackson asked then that I should be assigned to his command.

When General Johnston came up to supersede Jackson, he came without any written authority from the Confederate Government. Jackson declined to turn the army over to him, and made him wait until he could get the orders from Richmond before he permitted him to assume command.

Some months afterwards when I asked Jackson what he would have done if Johnston had insisted upon taking command without proper authority, he smiled and said, "I would have put him in the guardhouse."

❖

In person Jackson was a tall man, six feet high, angular, strong, with rather large feet and hands. . . . He rather strided along as he walked, taking long steps and swinging his body a little. There was something firm and decided, however, even in his gait. His eyes were dark blue, large, and piercing. He looked straight at you, and through you almost, as he talked. His nose was aquiline, his nostrils thin and mobile. His mouth was broad, his lips very thin. Generally they were compressed. He spoke in terse, short sentences, always to the point. There was never any circumlocution about what he had to say. His hair was brown and inclined to auburn. His beard was brown. He was as gentle and kind as a woman to those he loved. There was sometimes a softness and tenderness about him that was very striking. Under every and all circumstances he never forgot that he was a Christian and acted up to his Christian faith unswervingly, and yet he was not a bigoted denominationalist.

At one time just before the fight at Chancellorsville [May 1-3, 1863] we were ordered to send to the rear all surplus baggage. All tents were discarded except those necessary for office duty. We were allowed at headquarters only one tent, and that to take care of the papers. A Catholic priest belonging to one of the Louisiana brigades sent up his resignation because he was not permitted to have a tent, which he thought necessary to the proper performance of his office [*perhaps for privacy when counseling soldiers or hearing confessions*].

I said to General Jackson that I was very sorry to give up [the father]; that he was one of the most useful chaplains in the service. He replied: "If that is the case he shall have a tent." And so far as I know this Roman Catholic priest was the only man in the corps who had one.

❖

. . . I remember an incident which happened in the [Shenandoah] Valley of Virginia while the troops were marching up the Valley turnpike.

As Jackson rode along with his staff he was accosted by a poor, plain country woman to know if he was "Mr. Jackson" and if the troops in the road were his "company." The army then probably consisted of thirty thousand men. It was of course made up of divisions, brigades, and regiments, and a great many companies, but this woman only knew that her son "John" belonged to Jackson's "company," and she expressed a great deal of surprise when General Jackson told her that he didn't know her boy. "What," she said, "don't you know John _____? He has been with you a year, and I brought him these socks and something to eat." She began to cry bitterly.

Some members of the staff were disposed to laugh, but Jackson stopped them, got down from his horse and tried to explain to the woman how it was impossible that he should know her son, a simple private in the ranks, but she persisted he must know him, and she must see him, and that she had spent a great deal of time in fixing these things for him. He asked her what county the boy came from. He sent for Colonel Alexander Swift ["Sandie"] Pendleton and asked him what companies were in his army from that county. He then sent three or four couriers to each one of the companies from that county, and found the boy and brought him to the woman, who gave him the presents she had for him.

❖

. . . [A]t Malvern Hill[, l]ate in the night of the last day's fight [July 1, 1862][,] I found Jackson asleep by the side of a tree and his faithful servant Jim [Lewis] making some coffee for him to be ready when he awoke. While I was there several general officers came up and said that their commands were mobilized [*that is, on the move, and so not able to present a united line of defense*], and that if McClellan made an attack in the morning they would have no organized force with which to resist him. It was proposed presently to wake General Jackson up, and someone made the attempt, but when he went to sleep he was the most difficult man to arouse I ever saw. I have seen his servant pull his boots off and remove his clothes without waking him up, and so here at Malvern Hill on this night it was almost impossible to arouse him. At last some one got him up into a sitting posture and held him there, and another one yelled into his ear something about the condition of our army, its inability to resist attack the next morning, etc. He answered: "Please let me sleep; there will be no enemy in the morning," and so it turned out.

❖

Talking about Jackson's propensity to sleep, I remember[,] after the battles of the Seven Days' Fight [June-July 1862] around Richmond[,] one Sunday we went to Dr. Hoge's church. [General Jackson] went to sleep soon after the service began and slept through the greater part of it. A man who can go to sleep under Dr. Hoge's preaching can go to sleep anywhere on the face of this earth. When the service was over the people climbed over the backs of pews to get near him, and the aisles became crowded and General Jackson embarrassed. Presently he turned to me and said: "Doctor, didn't you say the horses were ready?" and I said, "Yes, sir," and we bolted from the church.

Many a night I have kept him on his horse by holding on to his coat-tail. He always promised to do as much for me when he had finished his nap. He meant to do it I am sure, but my turn never came.

It was told that at a council of war held by Lee, Longstreet and Jackson, that the last named went fast to sleep, and when roused and dimly conscious that his opinion was [being] asked he cried out: "Drive them into the river!"

When General Gregg, of South Carolina, was shot at Fredericksburg [December 13, 1862], an interesting incident occurred. General Jackson had had some misunderstanding with Gregg--what it was I have forgotten; but the night after this gallant soldier and splendid gentleman was mortally wounded, I told General Jackson, as I usually did, as far as I knew, of friends and prominent men killed and wounded. I had gotten to headquarters right late and found the General awake. Among others I mentioned General Gregg's case. [General Jackson] said: "I wish you would go back to see him. Tell him I want you to see him." I demurred a little, saying it had not been very long since I had seen him; that he was mortally wounded and that there was nothing to be done for him. He said: "I wish you would go see him; tell him I sent you." So I mounted my horse and rode to the Yerby house and saw General Gregg, who was slowly getting worse, and delivered the message. I had hardly gotten out of the room into the hall when I met General Jackson, who must have ridden very close behind me to have reached there so soon. He stopped me, asked about General Gregg, and went into the room to see him. No one else was in the room. What passed between the officers no one will ever know.

❖

Coarseness and vulgarity from anybody under any circumstances he would not brook. Swearing jarred upon him terribly and he generally reproved the man. Under some circumstances I have seen him forgive it and not notice it. I remember when the gallant General Trimble was a brigadier-general he expected and thought he ought to be a major-general, but when the appointments came out he was disappointed. I heard him talking about it to General Jackson one night. [General Trimble] was wrought up into a state of great indignation from his disappointment, and turning to General Jackson he said: "By G__, General Jackson, I will be a major-general or a corpse before this war is over!" Whatever Jackson thought he made no reproof.

I was once attending Major Harman, who was chief quartermaster. He was very sick for a day or two. General Jackson was anxious about him. One day in coming out of Harman's quarters I met the General, who was standing, waiting to see me. He said: "Doctor, how is Harman today?" I said: "He must be better, for he is swearing again." General Jackson gave Harman such a lecture next day that Colonel Pendleton advised me to keep out of Harman's way, as he swore he was going to shoot me.

He caught Lindsay Walker swearing once under circumstances that he did not reprove him. It was at Cedar Run [August 9, 1862]. The left wing of our army was commanded by Winder, and soon after the engagement began Winder was killed, and our troops on that side were pushed so hard that they broke and ran. General Walker had his battalion of artillery in the road; it was impossible to turn them around and get them out of the way, and they were in great danger of being captured. So Walker tried to rally the men and form a new line of battle. He would get a few men together, leave them to rally some others, and find that his first squad was gone. He was swearing outrageously. He had his long sword out and was riding up and down the little straggling line that he had when Jackson rode up. The latter had seen the disaster from his point of observation, and had come over to correct it if possible. On his way he ordered the Stonewall Brigade, which had been left in reserve, at a "double quick," but rode on in front of them to the scene of the trouble. He had lost his hat in the woods, and had his sword out. It was the only time I ever saw him with his sword out in battle. As soon as Walker saw him he stopped swearing. General Jackson, apparently simply conscious that Walker was using his efforts to rally the men, said: "That's right, General; give it to them." General Walker continued his work in his own way.

I was one day moving some wounded from the church in Port Republic, men who had been hurt when Ashby was killed, just before the battle of Port Republic [June 9, 1862], when the enemy sent two pieces of artillery close up to the town and began shelling the village. They fired at the church steeple, as the most prominent point, and it was difficult for me to make the wagoners and ambulance drivers wait until the wounded were put in these conveyances. I was riding up and down the line of wagons and ambulances, swearing at the men in a right lively manner. I did not know that General Jackson was in a mile or two of me, when I felt his hand upon my shoulder and he quietly asked me: "Doctor, don't you think you could get along without swearing?" I told him I would try, but I did not know whether I would accomplish it or not.

His habits of life were very simple. He preferred plain, simple food and generally ate right heartily of it. Corn bread and butter and milk always satisfied him. He used no tobacco and rarely ever drank any whiskey or wine. One bitter cold night at Dam No. 5, on the Potomac River [December 1861], when we could light no fire because of the proximity of the enemy, I gave him a drink of whiskey. He made a wry face swallowing it, and I said to him: "Isn't the whiskey good?" He answered: "Yes, very; I like it, and that's the reason I don't drink it."

. . . [General Jackson] did hold one, and only one, council of war. In March, 1862, at Winchester, Jackson had in his small army less than 5,000 men. Gen. Banks, who was advancing upon Winchester from Harper's Ferry and Charlestown [Charles Town], had 30,000 soldiers. Gen. Jackson repeatedly offered Gen. Banks battle, but the latter declined, and on the night of the 11th of March went into camp four miles from Winchester. Gen. Jackson sent for his officers and proposed to make a night attack, but the plan was not approved by the council. He sent for the officers a second time, some hours later, and again urged them to make the night assault, but they again disapproved of the attempt. So, late in the afternoon, we withdrew from Winchester and marched to Newtown. I rode with the General as we left the place, and as we reached a high point overlooking the town, we both turned to look at Winchester, just evacuated and now left to the mercy of the Federal soldiers.

I think that a man may sometimes yield to overwhelming emotion, and I was utterly overcome by the fact that I was leaving all that I held dear on earth, but my emotion was arrested by one look at Jackson. His face was fairly blazing with the fire that was burning in him, and I felt awed before him. Presently he cried out with a manner most savage: "That is the last council of war I will ever hold!" And it was--his first and last. Thereafter he held council in the secret chambers of his own heart.

❖

A short time before the battle of Second Manassas

SOUTHERN GENERALS

The generals starting at 12 o'clock and going clockwise are P.G.T. Beauregard, J. Longstreet, J.E.B. Stuart (sometimes spelled "Stewart," as on this engraving, and "Steuart"), A.S. Johnston, A.P. Hill, R.S. Ewell, and in the middle T.J. Jackson.

[August 28-30, 1862], there came from [Lexington] to join the Liberty Hall Volunteers a fine lad, whose parents, living [in Lexington], were dear friends of General Jackson. The General asked him to stop at his headquarters for a few days before joining his company, and he slept and messed [*that is, took meals*] with us. We all became much attached to the young fellow, and Jackson, in his gentle, winning way, did his best to make him feel at home and at ease; the lad's manners were so gentle, kindly and diffident, and his beardless, blue-eyed, boyish face so manly and so handsome. Just before the battle he reported for duty with his company. The night of the day of the great battle I was telling the General of the wounded, as we stood over a fire where black Jim, his servant, was making some coffee. I mentioned many of the wounded and their condition, and presently, calling by name the lad we all loved, told him that he was mortally wounded. Jim, faithful, brave, big-hearted Jim, God bless his memory! rolled on the ground, groaning in his agony of grief; but the General's face was a study. The muscles were twitching convulsively and his eyes were all aglow. He gripped me by the shoulders till it hurt me, and in a savage, threatening manner asked why I left the boy. In a few seconds he recovered himself, and turned and walked off into the woods alone. He soon came back, however, and I continued my report of the wounded and the dead. We were still sitting by the fire, drinking the coffee out of our tin cups, when I said: "We have won this battle by the hardest kind of fighting." And he answered me very gently and softly: "No, no; we have won it by the blessing of Almighty God." ♦

JUNE 1861: JUST BEFORE MANASSAS
BY
JOHN NEWTON LYLE

We had often seen our commander, Colonel T.J. Jackson, on the streets, at public gatherings and resisting sleep during Sunday services in the Presbyterian church at Lexington, but this was our first experience of him in the field. He was the least pretentious in dress of any of the field officers; a stranger . . . would not have picked out the man in the faded, blue-cloth coat, sunburnt, cadet-cap, no insignia to mark his rank, and poking around on the poorly caparisoned [*ornamented*] plug as the leader of the host. Nor would he have selected him as the material out of which to make a "Stonewall Jackson," nor would he have marked him as the one the war would develop into the greatest general that has arisen since Napoleon the First.

With the visor of his cap pulled down over his eyes, leaving no part of his face visible but that covered by a full, brown beard, and his huge feet thrust to the ankles into his stirrups, he rode about alone and had a far-away look on him, as if oblivious of his surroundings. It wouldn't have been wholesome, however, to have acted on the notion that he hadn't his eye on all around him.

I tested him [one] morning . . . to see if he knew where he was. He was riding along a country road, alone and with his far-away look on, and I was footing it along a path some hundred yards to his right, in a field. I waited till he was abreast of if not a little past me when I touched my cap-peak giving him the regulation salute. "Catch a weasel asleep, will you?" [he said,] instantly return[ing] the courtesy, convincing me that anywhere within "Old Jack's" horizon, whether to his front, flank, or rear, was a good place to behave yourself. ♦

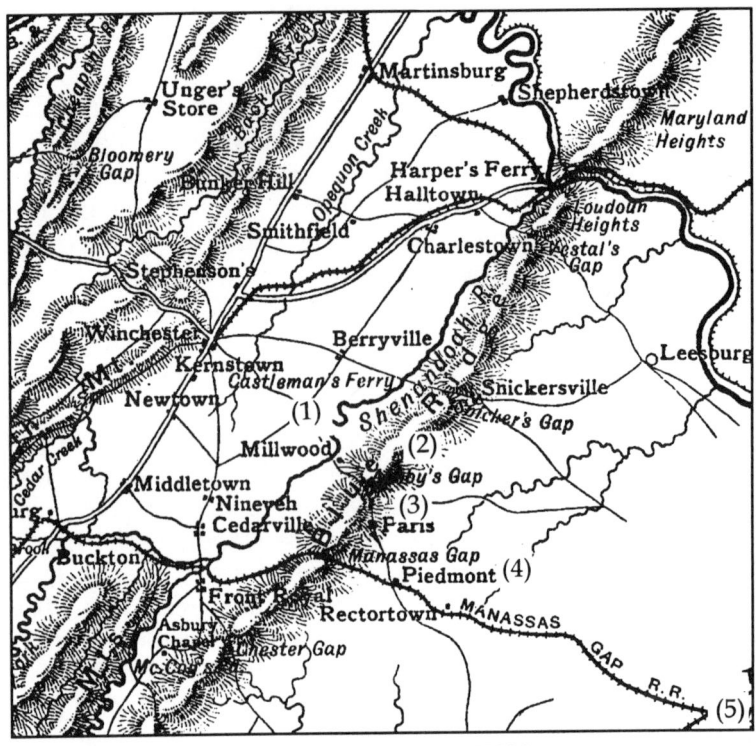

TO MANASSAS JUNCTION

Jackson's troops left Winchester marching fully equipped, and moving toward the Shenandoah River (1), forded it and then began the steep climb over the Blue Ridge at Ashby's Gap (2) at midnight, reaching the eastern side and stopping at Paris (3) at two in the morning. At daybreak they left for Piedmont Station — now Delaplane — (4) for railroad cars to Manassas Junction (5).

LET OUR MEN SLEEP
BY
JOHN NEWTON LYLE
AND
COLONEL JOHN T.L. PRESTON
JACKSON'S "PRINCIPAL ASSISTANT"
(CHIEF OF STAFF)

The famous "Lone Sentry" story told about General Jackson has been recounted not only in prose, but also in poetry, song and painting. The incident which it relates is said to have taken place in the early hours of July 18, 1861, just days before the Battle of First Manassas, as Jackson's troops were hard-marching toward the place where that battle would be fought. They had left Winchester fully equipped, and moving toward the Shenandoah River forded it, and then near midnight began the steep climb over the Blue Ridge at Ashby's Gap, reaching the eastern side about two AM. Having driven the men of his brigade almost beyond their endurance, Jackson found them totally exhausted when they made camp that night outside the small Virginia town of Paris. When told his guards had fallen asleep before being called out, it is said he stood watch alone, letting the troops sleep. In later years defenders of Jackson's memory have denied this incident could have happened, that a brilliant and conscientious military man would take it upon himself to stand a lone watch over a camp of some 2,600 troops within marching distance of the enemy.

And yet the strongest evidence indicates that it is a true story. Jackson's own words in a letter to his wife Mary Anna seem to verify it:

> "... [A]bout two o'clock in the morning we arrived at the little village of Paris, where we remained sleeping until nearly dawn. I mean the troops slept, as my men were so exhausted that I let them sleep while I kept watch myself."

Mary Anna's later elaboration on the information in that letter also stands as witness:

> "After pacing around the camp, or leaning upon the fence, watching the slumbers of his men until nearly daylight, he yielded his post to a member of his staff, who insisted on relieving him, and he then threw his wearied frame down upon a bed of leaves in a fence corner and snatched an hour or two of sleep."

"Bright and early," Jackson wrote his wife, "we resumed the march, and the head of our column arrived at Piedmont [now Delaplane], on the Manassas Gap Railroad, about six o'clock in the morning."

Jackson apparently had been assured that there was no imminent danger to his men. To understand how he might have felt this way when the Federals were in the area, it is helpful to read the words of Amanda Virginia Edmonds, a young Virginian who wrote in her diary on July 18, 1861, that "at tea" word came that Jackson's army was coming from Winchester and that she and her female friends were to go to Paris where they found that the "advance guard" had already arrived. "An hour or two after," Amanda wrote, "the army began to pour into Paris." She added that they "poured through all night and everybody in town and country was cooking and could not begin to satisfy the craving hunger of a third, though we were cooking hard and fast as fire and hands could do it."

The following day, July 19, 1861, Amanda recorded that the day had begun "amid bustle, excitement and confusion--rendering every service in our power to our dear, worn, fatigued soldiers." She saw "Regiment after Regiment . . . both Cavalry and Infantry." There was, she wrote, "an immense crowd." And she told about their "singing, laughing, and chatting." There were hundreds of men and "hundreds of wagons" in the little town.

It is understandable, then, that in this instance Jackson might not have seen a need for a strict adherence to the military rule which called for sentries in camp. With immense crowds of soldiers and townspeople milling about all night in the area where his men were sleeping, one lone sentry-- especially if he were General Jackson himself--would be sufficient.

John Lyle provides his own account of the march to Paris and the night spent there--which was for him personal experience--and with it another possibility: perhaps, he seems to indicate in the selection below, the guards who normally would have been posted under such circumstances were primarily needed to keep the men from leaving camp or otherwise causing trouble. Jackson seems to have concluded that his men were too tired to do anything but sleep after their long and tiring march.

. . . Ashby's [G]ap swallowed us into its darkness that night. All the illusions lent by distance were gone, and rocks and gulches all unclothed stood out in their naked ugliness. They called it a gap, where we crossed, but it was but a slight sway-back in the mountain. . . .

A little after midnight, we filed into an enclosure at

the roadside, and tumbled down for sleep. A depression in the ground, that fit me like a glove, fell to my lot as bed, and I knocked off a few happy hours of unconsciousness. The morning light revealed the fact that my couch was the sunken grave of a mortal long dead and buried. We were at Paris, a very small hamlet for so pretentious a name, and in the darkness our company had fallen on its cemetery as a bivouac. . . . .

It was at this halt that General Jackson told the officer of the day not to mount the guard, but to let the men rest, and that he would watch whilst the brigade slept. . . . The brigade was tired enough to sleep without watching [*that is, without being watched*], and the general had just as well taken his rest. . . . [Jackson] had better have put on guard one of his staff who had been riding all day whilst the men walked, [b]ut he was too considerate of others to make a lazy aide get out and do something unusual. Yet either of them [*i.e., Jackson or one of his aides*] were [*sic*] in a better condition to act as sentry, than men who had footed it twenty-two miles since noon, wading a river and climbing a mountain en route.

--JOHN NEWTON LYLE

Further evidence of the veracity of the reports of Jackson's action that July night in Paris can be found in the words of his friend Colonel Preston, spoken before the General Assembly and printed in the Wednesday Morning, June 3, 1863, LEXINGTON GAZETTE--*soon after Jackson's death.*

Colonel John T.L. Preston was a prominent citizen of Lexington and a great friend to Jackson as well as his chief of staff during the first months of the Civil War. Preston's second wife, Margaret ("Maggie"), was the sister of Jackson's first wife, Elinor, and the Jacksons, the Junkins, and the Prestons remained close even after "Ellie's" death and Jackson's remarriage. Indeed, the death of the Prestons' son Willie at Second Manassas was a great personal blow to Stonewall.

In his speech (which appears in part below), Colonel Preston related what he himself called "an incident characteristic" of "our beloved Jackson." Because he respected and loved his friend as much as he did, we may safely assume that he chose carefully, presumably with a keen regard for truth, the words he used to have Stonewall remembered by for all time.

I rise, sir, to place my broken utterances among the tributes to the hero. But, sir, I can hardly trust myself, for we were brothers in the church. And long before I shared the fatigues of the service with him and slept by his side in bivouac, often and often have we knelt together in prayer. I cannot speak, sir, and yet I cannot keep silent. . . .

. . . God has given us a great victory, and [yet] the people kneel and weep. . . . . . .

Will the Assembly pardon me, Mr. Moderator, for narrating an incident that is characteristic of him. At the battle of Manassas the victory was decided in our favor by the co-operation of the armies of Johns[t]on and Beauregard. Johns[t]on's army leaving their camps, leaving their foe in front of them suddenly crossed the mountains, and by his forced marches first gained for Jackson's troops the name of foot cavalry. Jackson, that night, ordered out his usual pickets, but the officer of the guard told him that the soldiers were all asleep completely exhausted--and asked whether he should arouse them. "No," replied the General, "let our men sleep. I will watch the camp," and silently he rode around that sleeping host, the only sentinel until the day broke in the east.

--COLONEL JOHN T.L. PRESTON

◆

GOING TO MANASSAS

Here Redwood depicts the 33d Virginia at Piedmont Station on its way to the Battle of First Manassas, July 21, 1861. At the station the Confederates boarded trains for the ride to Manassas Junction.

A. C. REDWOOD

COURTESY MUSEUM OF THE CONFEDERACY, RICHMOND, VIRGINIA
PHOTOGRAPH BY KATHERINE WETZEL

MAJOR GENERAL THOMAS JONATHAN "STONEWALL" JACKSON

This portrait of Jackson was painted in England in 1862 by Benjamin Franklin Reinhart, an American. Reinhart may have based his likeness of Jackson on a sketch that appeared in *The London Illustrated News* in December of 1862 (see page 126) or from a *carte de visite* of the 1851 photograph of Jackson (see page 24).

PART III

"STONEWALL"

FIRST MANASSAS

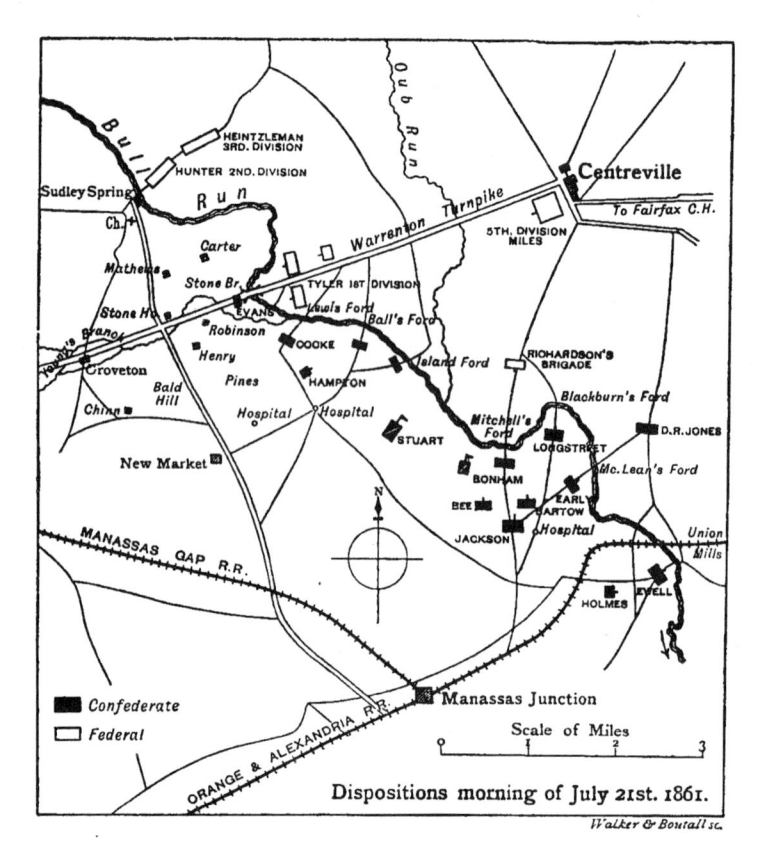

At First Manassas (First Bull Run) on July 21, 1861, Jackson rode up and down the line and cried out three times, "All's well; the First Brigade will have those guns! We will drive them across the Potomac tonight!" In less than thirty minutes his prediction was literally fulfilled. The brigade had the enemy in full retreat toward Washington and Jackson had gained the name "Stonewall."

LIKE A STONE WALL
BY
AN ANONYMOUS REPORTER
FOR THE
CHARLESTON MERCURY

General Barnard E. Bee had been with Jackson at West Point--a fellow cadet-- and was with him also at the first major battle of the Civil War, First Manassas (July 21, 1861), where the dark-eyed, long-haired general from South Carolina uttered his famous battle cry.

General Bee fell on the field soon after he called on his men to support Jackson, but by then his brigade had already responded to their courtly commander. Jackson held his position; then, supported by Bee's men, attacked--and the tide of battle was turned in favor of the Confederates.

It is generally understood that no one recorded verbatim the words General Bee called out to his troops that day, words that were to become almost as well known as the man they described. But only four days after First Manassas the following account appeared in the CHARLESTON MERCURY.

... [O]verwhelmed by superior numbers, and compelled to yield before a fire that swept everything before it, General Bee rode up and down his line, encouraging his troops, by everything that was dear to them, to stand up and repel the tide that threatened them with destruction. At last his own brigade dwindled to a mere handful, with every field officer killed or disabled. He rode up to General Jackson and said, "General, they are beating us back."

The reply was: "Sir, we'll give them the bayonet." General Bee immediately rallied the remnant of his brigade, and his last words to them were: "There is Jackson standing like a stone wall. Let us determine to die here and we will conquer. Follow me!"

CHARLESTON MERCURY, *July 25, 1861*

WHAT GENERAL BEE SAID AND DID
BY
WILLIAM M. ROBINS
MAJOR
FOURTH ALABAMA REGIMENT

Years after the end of the Civil War, Major Robins felt the need to set the record straight as to the exact nature of the words General Bee spoke to his men, among them Robins, on July 21, 1861.

. . . Our Brigadier-General Bee came galloping to the Fourth Alabama and said: "My brigade is scattered over the field, and you are all of it now at hand. Men, can you make a charge of bayonets?" Those poor, battered, and bloody-nosed Alabamians, inspired by the lion-like bearing of that heroic officer, responded promptly, "Yes, General, we will go wherever you lead, and do whatever you say." Bee then said, pointing to where Jackson and his men were so valiantly battling about a quarter of a mile to the west and left of us, "*Yonder stands Jackson like a stone wall. Let us go to their assistance.*" Saying this, he dismounted, placed himself at the left of the Fourth Alabama, and led the regiment (what remained of them) to Jackson's position and joined them on his right.

Some other reinforcements coming up, a vigorous charge was made, pressing the Federals back. In this charge Bee fell mortally wounded, leading the Fourth Alabama. . . . All the world knows how the Federals shortly thereafter were seized with a panic and fled . . . from the field.

It is not true that General Bee said, "[R]ally behind the Virginians," or anybody else. It is not true he was rallying his men at all, for they were not retiring. The glory of the Stonewall Brigade does not need to be enhanced by any deprecation of the equal firmness and heroism of other men on that historic field. Let it never be forgotten that the Fourth Alabama lost more men on that day than any other regiment but one in the Confederate army, and every field from there to Appomattox was moistened with the blood of her heroes. But several of them still survive to corroborate to the letter, [this] statement.... ♦

GENERAL JACKSON AT MANASSAS
The Stonewall Jackson Monument at Manassas
"... [H]e ... inspired confidence in his troops. There was a granite solidarity in his appearance that told you he would do to tie to."
– *JOHN NEWTON LYLE*

THE STONEWALL BRIGADE
BY
JOHN NEWTON LYLE

... [H]ere I had as well tell you something of the brigade [Jackson] led [at First Manassas], and from that day and from that occasion taking the name of "Stonewall," [which] lives in history inextricably linked with the fame of its great commander. Composed of five regiments, each mustering nearly a thousand muskets, and made up of the flower of the young men of the Valley and Southwest Virginia, it was a command worthy of such a commander. In the first year of the war, before the ranks were decimated, it was indeed a sight to see those gallant regiments in grey as they moved to battle, with glistening bayonets and Virginia's banner unfurled above them.

> To hero born for martial strife,
> Or bard for martial lay,
> 'Twere worth ten years of peaceful life
> One glance at their array.

There were privates in its ranks that could while away their leisure hours with Homer's Epics or the love songs of Horace, read fluently in the dead tongues in which they were written. . . .

Its devotion to Jackson was akin to idolatry. It is true, the men . . . swore hard at him for his swift marches. But this was a privilege they claimed as belonging strictly to themselves. A soldier of another command dared not indulge in the privilege in their presence. ♦

A. J. VOLCK

JACKSON
Ca. 1861

"He walked with head erect, chin thrown out, body inclined forward and eyes square to the front. From this right direction it looked as if no force could swerve him. . . . In battle . . . he was unmoved, bullets nor shot nor shell passing never so closely could gain recognition from him. . . ."

– JOHN NEWTON LYLE

STONEWALL JACKSON UNDER THE TABLE
BY
ANONYMOUS

When he was tired enough, Stonewall Jackson could and did fall asleep almost anywhere--on horseback, in church, even in the middle of a conversation. The narrator of this unsubstantiated (there being no other available evidence) anecdote about Stonewall Jackson is unknown, but a good guess is that he was from the North, for he calls the Battle of First Manassas "Bull Run," and refers to the Confederates as the "rebel army." Although not present himself when the incident occurred, he retells the major's story well.

Not long after the [B]attle of Bull Run[,] a certain major . . . of the rebel army called on General Joe Johnston at his headquarters in Virginia, arriving just in time for dinner, which was served in . . . General [Johnston's] tent. When the meal was nearly finished, there was a movement under the table and something very like a yawn came from beneath it, the major at the time feeling something heavy roll on his feet. Raising the cloth General Johnston looked down and remarked, laughing: "Jackson smells the dinner at last; I know he must be nearly famished."

"It was the only time I ever saw Stonewall Jackson," says the major. "He had been without sleep for three days when he reached Johnston's tent, and tumbling down in the center of it, the table was set over him." ♦

ASLEEP IN A SECOND
BY
CHARLES MINOR BLACKFORD
CAPTAIN, COMPANY B
SECOND VIRGINIA CAVALRY

Charles Blackford was married and the father of three young children when the Civil War began. Though his two-year-old son and one of his small daughters died during the war, Charles lived through it and came home to practice law, work for the railroad, and live a long life.

His letters to his wife, Susan Leigh Blackford, who remained in the family home in Lynchburg, Virginia, for most of the war, were published by her privately--"to preserve" the story--and later publicly by her grandson Charles M. Blackford III. The portion excerpted below from the letter Captain Blackford wrote home on August 2, 1862, contains another description of Stonewall Jackson asleep.

. . . Day before yesterday I was riding with Jackson and his staff investigating some roads which I suppose he expects to use. We had not ridden more than five or six miles, and it was not more than two o'clock in the day, when the General suddenly stopped and dismounted at the foot of a tree, unbuckled his sword and stood it by the tree and then la[y] down with his head on the root of the tree and was asleep in a second, or appeared to be so. I was amazed and glanced at the other gentlemen, who I thought were not so much surprised. The General had not said a word as he went to rest and we were equally quiet while he slept. He la[y] with his eyes shut about five or six minutes, got up, buckled on his sword, mounted and rode on without any explanation or comment. Was not that a curious freak? He is a curious, wonderful man. No one seems to know much about him, not even those who are with him hourly. He has no social graces, but infinite earnestness. ♦

SKETCHES OF STONEWALL
BY
GIDEON DRAPER CAMDEN

The sketch of Stonewall Jackson on the left of the page opposite was drawn December 13, 1862, in the evening after the day's fighting at Fredericksburg, by Alexander Galt, sculptor, artist and soldier in the CSA army, who was making sketches of Jackson in preparation for a bust of the general. Galt died of smallpox on January 19, 1863, at the age of 36--presumably before the bust could be completed. The sketch on the right was done by Colonel Alexander Robinson Boteler, Virginian, former United States congressman and member of the CSA legislature. Boteler had a close personal relationship with Jackson and eventually became part of his staff.

The letter below was written from Brownsburg, Virginia, on November 25, 1863, by Judge Gideon Draper Camden, one of Jackson's old friends from (now West) Virginia, to Dr. Robert Lewis Dabney, a theologian whom Jackson had, for a while, made his adjutant general and unofficial chief of staff. (Note that Boteler was present when Galt made his sketch of Jackson.)

The next time I saw the Genl. was at his headquarters near Fredericksburg on Monday evening after the great battle there. Governor Letcher and the lamented M. Galt went up on the train on Monday morning after the fight. I accompanied them and in the evening we went to his headquarters. Found Mr. Boteler there. It was expected that the battle would be renewed the next morning. We remained with the general during the night. M. Galt requested Governor Letcher to ask permission of the General to take his likeness which was gained and shortly after dark Mr. G. commenced, the Genl. sitting bettween Mr. G. and myself at a stand or table. While Mr. G. was operating with his pencil a conversation was continued principally between the Genl. and myself for some 15 or 20 minutes, when he fell into a profound sleep sitting in his seat and continued to sleep about 20 minutes before waking up. ♦

COURTESY MANUSCRIPTS AND OLD BOOKS,
SWEM LIBRARY, WILLIAM AND MARY COLLEGE
STONEWALL JACKSON,
DECEMBER 13, 1862
Sketch by A. Galt

COURTESY SPECIAL COLLECTIONS DEPARTMENT,
TRACY W. MCGREGOR LIBRARY, UNIVERSITY OF VIRGINIA
STONEWALL JACKSON,
JULY 29, 1862
Sketch by A. Boteler

I WISH I COULD GO WITH HIM
BY
HUGH AUGUSTUS WHITE
PRIVATE, LIBERTY HALL VOLUNTEERS
FOURTH VIRGINIA REGIMENT
STONEWALL BRIGADE

Hugh Augustus White, the son of Jackson's esteemed friend and minister Dr. William S. White of the Presbyterian church in Lexington, entered Washington College in 1854, when he was only 14 years old. In his senior year he was tutor of both Latin and mathematics, and at the age of 18 he graduated with distinction, receiving one of the gold medals given to the top three scholars.

In 1861 Hugh began his soldier's life as a private under the command of his older brother, James J. White, captain of the Liberty Hall Volunteers (and professor of Greek at Washington College); at the time, the men of the LHV were under the direct command of Stonewall Jackson, the LHV being part of his brigade. When Jackson left the Stonewall Brigade to take an independent command in the Valley, his men were left behind, much to Hugh's disappointment, as the letter below to his father reveals.

Centerville, October, 1861

My dear father:

I do not think that any man can take General Jackson's place in the confidence and love of his troops. I wish I could go with him, though my hardships would be more than doubled. I have learned to look up to him with implicit confidence, and to approach him with perfect freedom, being always assured of a kind and attentive hearing. . . .

Within a short time the Stonewall Brigade was transferred to Jackson's new command and Hugh White served once again under Jackson. Once again he wrote to his father about his commander.

COURTESY SPECIAL COLLECTIONS, LEYBURN LIBRARY,
WASHINGTON & LEE UNIVERSITY

CAPTAIN HUGH WHITE

Liberty Hall Volunteers, Fourth Virginia Regiment

"True to the traditions of their alma mater, [Washington College], to the memory of their brave ancestors and the honor of the state, the students of 1861 organized under the name The Liberty Hall Volunteers at the first alarm of war and joined Jackson at Winchester. . . . Jackson's interest in these boys was that of a father."

– *JOHN NEWTON LYLE*

Feb. 5, 1862

... There is but one feeling with us--that of perfect devotion to Gen. Jackson. With him we are ready to go anywhere, and to endure anything. ...

Hugh continued to be promoted and had reached the rank of captain in the Fourth Virginia when he was killed leading his troops into action at Second Manassas in August 1862. In a letter to a friend, Jackson wrote, "In the second battle of Manassas I lost more than one personal friend."

FIRST NATIONAL FLAG OF THE CONFEDERACY

This flag, with its seven stars representing the first seven states to secede, was first "raised over the state capitol at Montgomery, Alabama, on March 4, [1861], by Miss Letitia Tyler, a granddaughter of the tenth president of the United States, John Tyler."

JACKSON UP A TREE
BY
JOHN NEWTON LYLE

Stonewall Jackson liked to eat fruit, and it appears that during the Civil War he developed a predilection for lemons--when they were available (the Union provided these imported "luxuries" to its soldiers; they were often enjoyed by the Confederate army as captured goods). Jackson was reportedly seen sucking on lemon halves on at least three occasions during the war; on another occasion, shortly after Christmas 1861, he wrote to his quartermaster, Major Harman, that he was "much obliged . . . for the nice lemons" the major had sent to him.

Jackson's "habit" of choosing the lemon may be attributed to his awareness of the effect of diet and the knowledge then available of the danger of scurvy and how to prevent it (British seamen used lemons and limes to prevent this disease and were, as a result, called "limeys"). It was also a common belief that lemons were good for dyspepsia, a condition from which Jackson was known to suffer. But since we know that his aide James Power Smith served him lemonade on his deathbed and that Stonewall complained then that it was too sweet, it seems possible that what the general especially liked was simply the taste of sour things. The following incident, which took place in November 1861 (soon after Jackson's promotion to major general), seems to attest to this.

Stonewall Jackson climbed into a persimmon tree and had to be helped down by his staff. . . . [He had an] appetite for such dainties as corndodger and green gooseberries. These are delicacies compared to persimmons in November, when they will pucker your mouth like that of a closed tobacco sack, till you can't tell whether you are whistling or singing. Even after the frosts and snows of winter have fallen on them they retain an amount of astringency that renders them unpalatable.

The General, tempted by this fruit as Eve was by the apple, practiced his boyish feat of tree-climbing and it got him into a place he couldn't get out of. This was more than Banks, Fremont and Shields could do on the same ground the following summer. ♦

HARD MARCHING
BY
SAM R. WATKINS
"HIGH" PRIVATE, COMPANY H
FIRST TENNESSEE REGIMENT

Although he was in general admired, Stonewall Jackson was not always and universally well thought of. He carried on a feud with his quartermaster, John Harman of Staunton; the men often resented the discipline--he would, one of them wrote, "have a man shot at the drop of a hat, and drop it himself"; and there were constant complaints from his men about the hard marching and the poor rations. In addition, General Ewell at first thought he was crazy; Winder thought he was cruel; and Taylor thought he was ambitious and merciless.

There is no doubt that Stonewall Jackson was a rigid disciplinarian, a commander hard on his troops both physically and sometimes spiritually, as attested to by words in a letter written home early in the war by one officer, who said, "Jackson is considered rigid to the border of tyranny by the men. . . ." Later, however, like many in Jackson's army, the same officer modified his opinion, writing home that ". . . General Jackson is rigid in his requirements, although not more so than security requires." In fact, the men eventually came to take a perverse pride in their strict commander and their hard life in his ranks, and the following saying became popular: "Man that is born of woman, and enlisteth in Jackson's army, is of few days and short rations."

Of the events relating to Jackson that the men complained most about, first of all was probably the disastrous Romney campaign--through which, among other goals, Stonewall had hoped to deny the Union the western part of Virginia. This expedition to Romney in the dead of winter resulted in much justified criticism on the part of Jackson's troops, from officer to private. The cold weather, the difficult terrain--made worse by ice and snow--caused almost 2,000 soldiers to fall ill. "Our confidence in our leader was sorely tried," wrote William Poague of the Rockbridge Artillery. "[One] part of the army was in a state of semi-mutiny and Jackson was hissed and hooted at as he passed by them."

Sam Watkins, from Tennessee, was on the march to Romney, and he remembered it well. Private Watkins was born June 26, 1839, "near Columbia, Tennessee," and attended Jackson College in Columbia. He joined a company of local boys, the Maury Grays, at the opening of the war in the spring of 1861, when he was 21 years old. This unit became Company H, First Tennessee Regiment, which was sent to the Shenandoah Valley and, shortly thereafter, assigned to Jackson's command--where the fate of the regiment, Sam said, was to be "ever on the march. . . ."

*The men in Sam's unit stayed with Jackson until early 1862, when they returned to Tennessee to fight in the western theater, better and tougher soldiers than they had been before their service with Stonewall. In the following passages from his memoir, "*CO. AYTCH,*" Private Sam Watkins tells of his first sight of Stonewall, in the fall of 1861, and then describes the hardships of what is known as the Romney campaign. Interestingly, Sam's opinion of Jackson was not much harmed by the hard marching and intense discipline he experienced in Jackson's army. "One secret of Stonewall's success," he wrote, "was that he was such a strict disciplinarian. He did his duty himself and was ever at his post and demanded of everybody to do the same thing."*

March, march, march; tramp, tramp, tramp, tramp, back through the valley . . . and up through the most beautiful valley--the Shenandoah--in the world, passing towns and elegant farms and beautiful residences, rich pastures and abundant harvests. . . . Passing on, we arrived at Winchester. . . .

[Here] is the first sight we had of Stonewall Jackson, riding up on his old sorrel horse, his feet drawn up as if his stirrups were much too short for him, and his old dingy military cap hanging well forward over his head, and his nose erected in the air, his old rusty sabre rattling by his side. This is the way the grand old hero of a hundred battles looked.

❖

Our march to and from Romney was in midwinter in the month of January, 1862. It was the coldest winter known to the oldest inhabitant of the region. . . . The soldiers on this march got very much discouraged and disheartened. As they marched along[,] icicles hung from their clothing, guns, and knapsacks; many were badly frost bitten, and I heard of many freezing to death along the road side. My feet peeled off like a peeled onion on that march. The snow and ice on the ground being packed by the soldiers' tramping, the horses hitched to the artillery wagons were continually slipping and sliding and falling and wounding themselves and sometimes killing their riders. The wind whistling with a keen and piercing shriek seemed as if [it] would freeze the marrow in our bones. The soldiers in the whole army got rebellious--almost mutinous--and would curse and abuse Stonewall Jackson; in fact, they called him "Fool Tom Jackson." They blamed him for the cold weather; they blamed him for everything, and when he would ride by a regiment they would take the occasion . . . to abuse him . . . [but] loud enough for him to hear. Soldiers from all commands would fall out of ranks and stop by the road side and swear that they would not follow such a leader any longer. ♦

STONEWALL JACKSON--A MEMORY
BY
ALLEN CHRISTIAN REDWOOD
PRIVATE, MIDDLESEX SOUTHRONS
55TH VIRGINIA REGIMENT

When the early details of the first important collision between the contending forces in Virginia, in 1861, began to come in, some prominence was given to the item relating how a certain brigade of Virginia troops, recruited mostly from the Shenandoah [V]alley and the region adjacent to the Blue Ridge, had contributed, largely by their steadiness under fire, almost for the first time, to the sustaining of the hard-pressed and wavering Confederate left flank, and the subsequent conversion of what had threatened to be a disastrous defeat to the Southern arms into a disorderly and utter rout of the opposing army.

War was a very new experience to most of that generation, and the capacity for absorbing sensational bulletins was commensurate with the popular expectation, if it did not exceed it. Those of us who were as yet doing the commonplace duty of detached garrisons, were consumed with envy of our more fortunate comrades who had taken part in what then seemed the great battle of the war and which our inexperience even conjectured might determine the pending issues. A man who had "been at Manassas" might quite safely draw upon his imagination to almost any extent in relating its happenings, with no fear that the drafts would not duly be honored by our credulity. As to the civilian element, its appetite was bounded only by the supply; like poor little Oliver Twist, it continually presented its porringer, eagerly demanding "more!"

Of this mass of fiction--of unthreshed grain--there remains yet one kernel of veracious history, and the incident was predestined to exercise significant and far-reaching influence upon the struggle, then in its very inception. In that fiery baptism, a man still unknown to fame was to receive, at the hands of a gallant soldier about to surrender his soul to the Maker who gave it, the name which, to the world, was to supplant that conferred by his natural sponsors, and which he will ever be known as among the great captains of his race and of history. The supreme effort of the Federal commander was directed against the left of the army of Johnston and Beauregard and upon the open plateau surrounding the Henry House. The battle was raging furiously, and seemingly the Southern line at that point was on the verge of utter disaster, when the [South] Carolinian, General Barnard E. Bee, rode from his shattered and wavering brigade over to where Jackson still held fast with his mountain men.

"General," he said in tones of anguish, "they are beating us back."

"No, sir," was the grim reply; "we will give them the bayonet." Bee rode back and spoke to his brigade: "Look at Jackson there, standing like a stone wall. Rally behind the Virginians!" and the front of battle was restored. The rest is history.

Thus it came to pass that popular inquiry began as to who this man Jackson might be, and what were his credentials and antecedents. The young cadets from the Virginia Military Institute, who promptly flocked to the colors of the State of the Confederacy, could give but little satisfactory information; to their boyish minds he was just "Old Jack," instructor in natural philosophy and artillery tactics, something of a martinet and stickler for observance of regulation, and, on the whole, rather "queer" and not at all approachable. That he should be in command of a brigade seemed to them due far more to some peculiar fortune

COURTESY VIRGINIA MILITARY INSTITUTE ARCHIVES
VMI DRILL FIELD

Though shown (Ca. 1900) some 45 years after Jackson taught artillery at the Virginia Military Institute, the drill field and guns in this picture are little changed from his day.

than to any inherent fitness residing in him. True, he was said to have graduated from the United States Military Academy, and was known to have been a some-time officer of the army, serving in Magruder's battery in Mexico during the campaign of Scott from Vera Cruz to the capital city.

It was even intimated that he had won certain brevets there for service at Vera Cruz, Contreras, and Chapultepec, within a period of eighteen months, but to the youthful sense all that was very ancient history . . . and the mists of antiquity hung about the record and made its outlines very vague. To the young, ten years seems a great while, and during that period their reticent, rigid instructor had been quite out of touch with everything military other than their cadet battalion or the gun details of the institute battery of 6-pounders, with human teams, which it was his duty to put through their evolutions on the drill-ground.

The human side of this man has almost no record during these years, apart from what comes through to us through the letters to his wife; he was not a man who wore his heart on his sleeve, and life seems to have always been to him a trust, for which he held himself strictly accountable, and which was not to be squandered in trivialities of any sort. As we know now, he had much to do, and the time for it was to be all too brief for its full accomplishment; yet he seems to have been not quite devoid of some sense of humor, in spite of his habitual reserve and aloofness.

It is related that upon one occasion, at this stage of his career, he propounded to his class this question, "Young gentlemen, can any of you explain to me the reason why it has never been possible to send a telegraphic dispatch from Lexington to Staunton?" Several theories were advanced, such as that the pressure of iron ore in the surrounding mountains might have had the effect of deflecting the electric current. At last, one boy--the dullard of the class, usually--suggested, diffidently, that it might be owing to the fact that there was no telegraph line then existing between the two points. "Yes, sir," replied Major Jackson; "that is the reason."

But, in the main, he was eminently practical and almost totally lacking in the minor graces and frivolities which render men socially possible, and, had not the great occasion arisen which was to afford scope for his ability, it seems as if he must have entirely escaped notice for the rest of his life. We are prone to look at things in that light, ignoring the fact that it is the man who has kept up his training who is ready and fit to seize opportunity when it shall present itself. Jackson had been "in training" all the while, even though no one--not even himself--may have suspected to what purpose.

This is the man who, more than any other, saved the day for the Confederacy at Manassas (First Bull Run), in 1861. Then he disappeared from view--a way he had, as his antagonists were to learn later--for a while, and at one time it seemed as if the theater of active operations was to know his presence no more, when, in response to an order from the War Department in Richmond, along with his acquiescence, he tendered his resignation from the command he then held.

Fortunately, this document went through the headquarters of his superior, General Joseph E. Johnston, who before forwarding it wrote to Jackson asking reconsideration, and so the services of the latter were retained to the Confederacy, and we were to hear much of his doings from that time until his untimely and tragic death. But in the months immediately succeeding Bull Run, he was almost lost sight of, and it was only at the opening of the campaign of 1862 that he began to loom again upon the military horizon.

The fortunes of the young Confederacy seemed then at a low ebb; from all the western portion came bulletins of disaster. In Virginia, a vast Federal host had been marshaled and was about to begin closing in upon the capital [at Richmond], and all the outlying posts of the Confedederate line were being severally driven in. Johnston had retired from Manassas to the line of the Rappahannock, presently to proceed to Yorktown, and eventually to retire thence to the Chickahominy. It was while lying there, awaiting McClellan's attack, that we began to get news of very active proceedings in the Valley region, which came to have important bearing upon our fortunes, and in the

A. C. REDWOOD

UNDER ARTILLERY ATTACK

final issue to determine the contest we were expecting and awaiting in our immediate front. To those sultry, squalid camps, reeking with malaria and swarming with flies, came from beyond the far-away Blue Ridge stirring and encouraging tidings of rapid march and sudden swoop; of telling blows where least expected; of skilful maneuvering of a small force, resulting in the frustrating of all combinations of one numerically superior, and paralyzing for the time being all the plans of the Federal War Department and the grand strategy of the "young Napoleon" [*McClellan*] at the head of its armies in the field.

It seemed as if the *sobriquet* conferred upon Manassas field had become the veriest of misnomers; the "Stonewall" had acquired a marvelous mobility since that July day not yet a year old and had become a catapult instead. And what, perhaps, appealed to our personal interest more forcibly was the story of the capture of the rich spoil of war, the supplies, of which we were already beginning to feel the need. Our daily diet of unrelieved bread and bacon grew fairly nauseating at the thought of the bounty so generously provided by "Commissary-General" Banks, and the extra dainties inviting pillage in the tents of Israel--but we were to get our share, with accrued interest, later on.

We had not yet ceased to marvel over these exploits when Jackson executed one of his mysterious dissappearances, puzzling alike to friend and foe, and he next announced himself by the salvo of his guns, driving in McClellan's exposed right. This exposed condition was due to his own activity in the Valley, which had held McDowell inert upon the Rappahannock with thirty-five thousand muskets which should have been with the force north of the Chickahominy, inviting attack. Jackson rarely declined such invitations; he could scent an exposed flank with the nose of a hound and was "fast dog" following the trail when struck. Besides his habitual celerity of movement, was his promptness in delivering attack, which was an element of his success.

"The first musket upon the ground was fired," says a distinguished English authority, "without giving the opposing force time to realize that the fight was on and to make its dispositions to meet the attack or even to ascertain in what force it was being made." The quiet, retiring pedagogue of the "V.M.I." had not been wasting those ten years in which most of his leisure had been devoted to the study of the campaigns of the greatest strategists of history, from Caesar to Napoleon, and his discipline in Mexico had given him some useful suggestions for their application to modern conditions. Also it had afforded the opportunity for giving that invaluable asset, the ability to ga[u]ge the caliber of the men cooperating with him or opposed to him, with most of whom he had come in contact personally--a peculiarity of our Civil War, and one of important bearing upon all the operations conducted by officers of the regular establishment who, almost without exception, held high command in both armies.

But as yet we had no personal knowledge of this man who had been so rapidly coming to the fore. His work done, and well done, amid the Chickahominy lowlands, he was soon to heed the call coming to him from the hill country which gave him birth, and where his most notable service had so far been rendered. His old antagonists were reassembling there as a formidable army and under a new leader, and the line of direct approach to the Confederate capital was to be attempted from that direction. Already he had proceeded thither with his two divisions which had made the Valley campaign--his own and Ewell's--when ours, commanded by A.P. Hill, received orders to join them, and all three were thenceforth incorporated in the Second Corps of the Army of Northern Virginia, as long as he commanded it.

We had fought the sharp engagement of Cedar Mountain on the 9th of August, 1862, and checked Pope's advance to the Rapidan. Then, after some days of rest, we again took the initiative and, crossing the little river, went after him. But the general who

A. P. HILL

72

had heretofore "seen only the backs of his enemies" did not see fit to await our coming, but made so prompt and rapid a retrograde movement that even our expeditious "foot cavalry" could not come up with him before he passed the Rappahannock. It was on this hurried pursuit, passing through Brandy Station, that a figure came riding along the toiling column toward the front. He was in no wise remarkable in appearance, and it was with surprise that the writer heard that he was no other than our commander, General "Stonewall" Jackson.

He wore a rather faded gray coat and cap to match, the latter of the "cadet" pattern then in vogue and tilted so far over his eyes that they were not visible, and his mount and general appearance were not distinctive of high rank. In fact, he seemed some courier carrying a message to some general officer on ahead. Despite his West Point training, he was never a showy horseman--in which respect he had a precedent in the great Napoleon. When we took Harper's Ferry, in September of that same year, one of the surrendered garrison remarked, when Jackson was pointed out to him, "Well, he's not much to look at, but if we'd only had *him*, we'd never had been in this fix."

But within the interval we were to see much of him, and our appreciation speedily penetrated below the surface indications as we came to know and trust the man who conducted us to unfailing victory. Soldiers always forgive the means so that the end may be assured, and no man ever worked his troops harder than did Jackson, or ever awakened in them more intense enthusiasm and devotion. His appearance never failed to call forth that tumultuous cheer which was part of the battle onset. This was mostly, it must be admitted, in a spirit of mischief and for the sake of "making 'Old Jack' run," for he never liked an ovation and always spurred out of the demonstration at top speed.

A. C. REDWOOD

CROSSING THE RAPIDAN

"We . . . checked Pope's advance to the Rapidan. Then, after a few days of rest, we again took the initiative and, crossing the little river, went after him."

– ALLEN CHRISTIAN REDWOOD

Rigid disciplinarian that he was in all essentials, there was not the suspicion of concern with pomp and circumstance in all his make-up. War was to him much too serious an affair to be complicated by anything of the sort, nor was he at all tolerant of excuses when there was work in hand--results alone counted.

At Chantilly, our division commander sent word to him that he was not sure that he could hold his position as his ammunition was wet. "My compliments to General Hill and say that the enemy's ammunition is as wet as his, and to hold his ground," was Jackson's reply. Yet, as unsparing as he was of his men when the urgency of the occasion demanded it, he was equally unsparing of himself, and, moreover, was always concerned for their well-being once the emergency was past, realizing that all warlike preparation is to the end of lavish expenditure at the supreme moment. In camp he was always solicitous that the troops should be well cared for, but when it came to take the field,

> *What matter if our shoes are worn,*
> *What matter if our feet are torn,*
> *Quick step--we're with him ere the dawn . . .*

That was "Stonewall Jackson's Way." A purposeful man, obstacles were to him but things to be overcome or ignored if they stood in the way of his plans. When one of his subordinates, after the three days' hard fighting of the Second Manassas, preceded by a march of almost a hundred miles within a little more than a like period of time, objected that his men could not march further until they should have received rations, he was promptly put under arrest by Jackson, bent as he was upon following up his advantage and overwhelming Pope's defeated army before it could reach the protection of its entrenched lines at Alexandria, some thirty miles distant.

A master of men, Jackson infused those of his command with much of his own indomitable spirit, as expressed in the lines quoted from the old songs of the corps, until they came to take pride in their hardships and privations and to profess a Spartan-like contempt for the sybaritic softness, as they considered it, of the other corps of the army. As to their confidence in his ability to meet and to dominate any situation, it simply had no bounds. In the movement on Manassas and during the engagement, with hostile forces coming from almost every direction, and while as yet we had no tidings of Longstreet, we were remote from our base and the foe was in superior force between; we were footsore and fagged nearly to the limit of human endurance, but there was no faltering in the belief that Jackson saw his way out of the toils which seemed to compass him about, as he had aforetime in the Valley campaign. Those thin lines never held their ground more tenaciously nor charged with more *elan* than during those eventful August days. ♦

&

THE PRINCE AND PRINCESS OF WALES WENT AFTER THEIR MARRIAGE TO OXFORD. THE CEREMONIES OF WELCOME WERE PERFORMED IN THE THEATRE, OR PUBLIC HALL, OF THE UNIVERSITY. THE YOUNG ENGLISHMEN [THE STUDENTS AT OXFORD UNIVERSITY] CHEERED FOR MR. DAVIS AND STONEWALL JACKSON AND GROANED FOR MR. LINCOLN.

--HARPER'S MONTHLY

IN THE SHENANDOAH VALLEY, 1862
BY
ANDREW DAVIDSON LONG
PRIVATE, COMPANY A
FIFTH VIRGINIA REGIMENT
STONEWALL BRIGADE

Andrew ("Andy") Davidson Long was 17 years old when he joined the Fifth Virginia of the Stonewall Brigade in the winter of 1861. As part of Company A he participated in many battles, among them McDowell, Franklin, Front Royal, Winchester, Brandy Station, Mine Run, and finally Spotsylvania Court House, where he was wounded and captured at the Bloody Angle (May 1864). He remained in a Union prison until the end of the war, after which he returned home to Rockbridge Baths (in Virginia), married, and then moved to Texas where he earned a prominent place among the citizens of Austin and the nickname "Honest Andy." Andy recounted his memories of the war to his son, and these were later written down for posterity by Andy's grandson, Walter E. Long.

After considerable training I went into my first battle commanded by General Jackson. This was the battle of McDowell. It was fought in May, 1862.

The Yankee Generals Banks, Fremont, and Milroy planned to throw Jackson back, crush the Stonewall Brigade and take over the rich country around Staunton. This would kill the Valley Pike, curtail rail lines, and shut off the lower Valley.

That wonderful cavalry leader, General Ashby, was protecting our rear as Jackson slowly moved away from Kernstown. . . .

Jackson often counter-marched his men to fool the Yankees. This he did before the battle of McDowell. He marched his men down the Valley south toward Richmond, letting the Yankees know this. Jackson was giving the impression that he was trying to cut Banks off from Richmond. He then counter-marched us back north up the

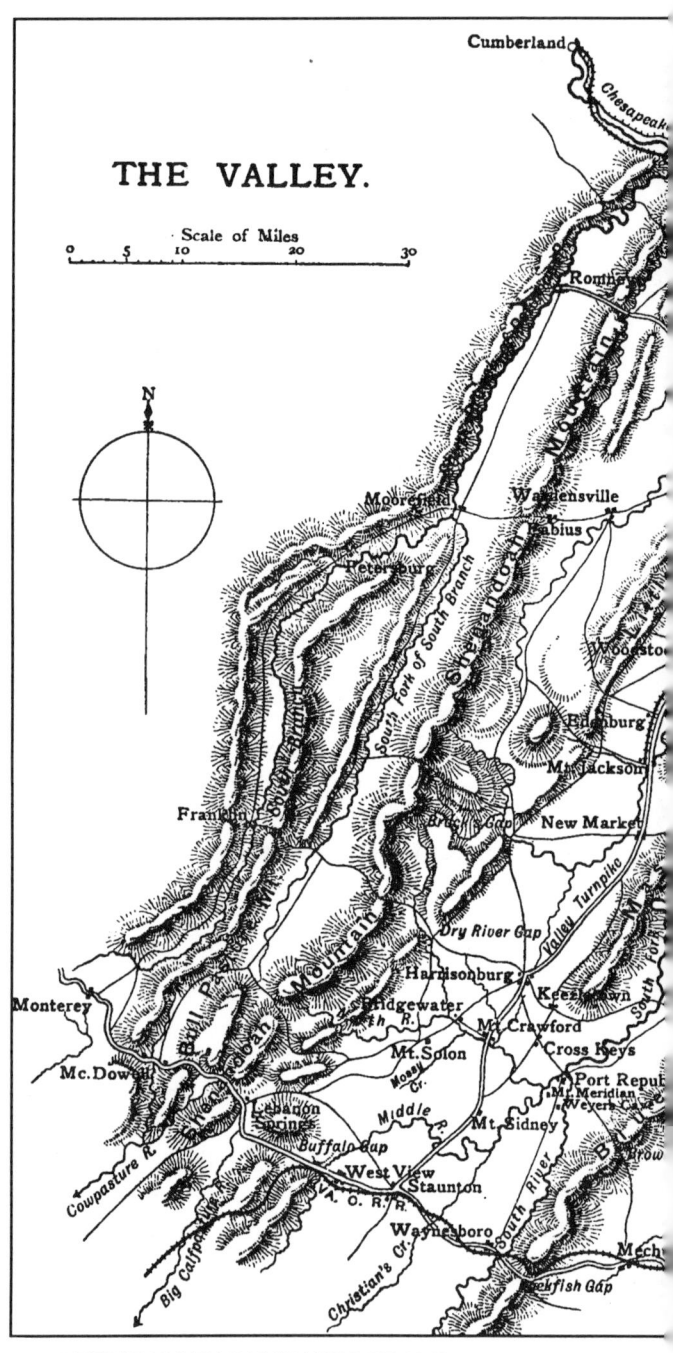

THE VALLEY CAMPAIGN OF 1862

In the spring of 1862 Jackson started a new campaign in the Valley. With maneuvering and speed reminiscent of Napoleon, Jackson whipped Milroy, Banks, Shields and Fremont in this campaign in the Valley, and suddenly appeared at Gaines' Mill (First Cold Harbor), when the United States authorities thought he was still in the Valley, constituting one of the most brilliant chapters in all modern warfare.

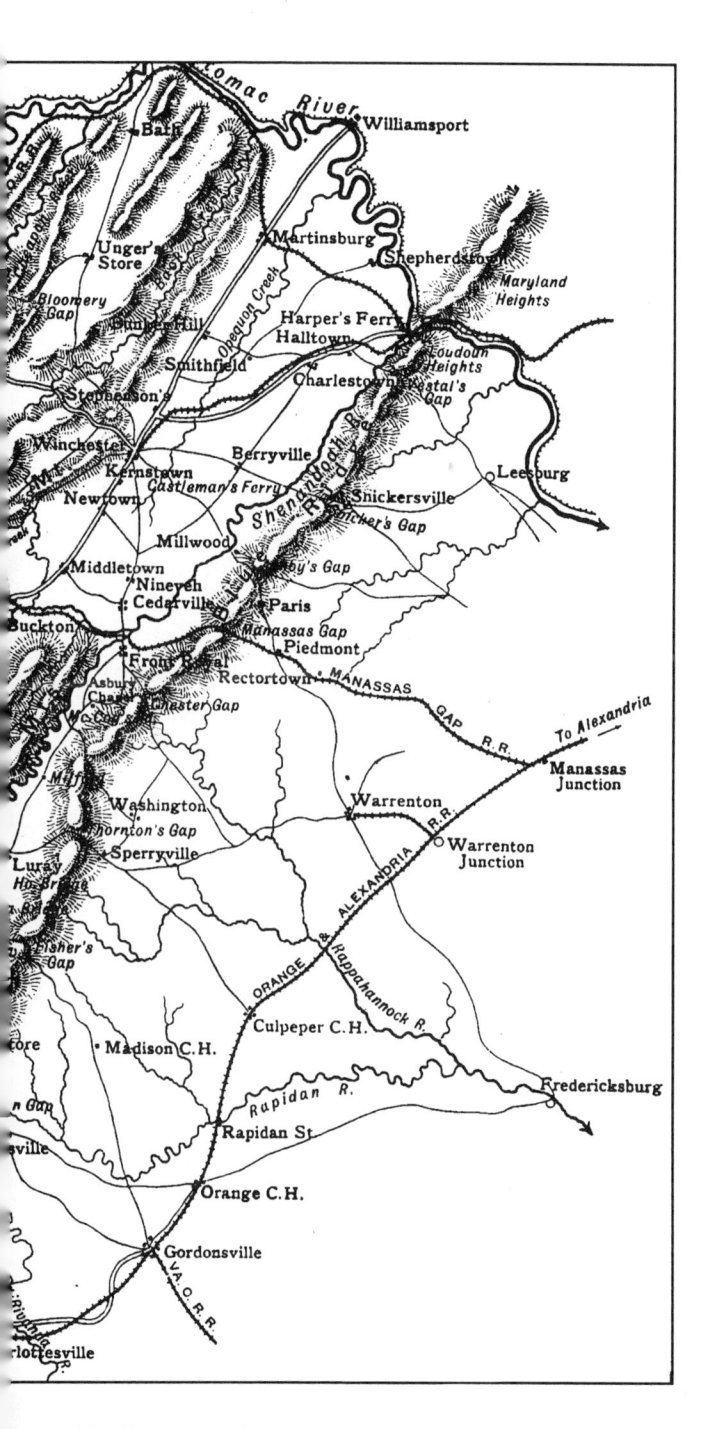

Valley without letting Banks know this. He cut across the Blue Ridge and came in behind Banks, scared his whole army which took to flight, and left great supplies of arms, food and clothing which we needed badly. The bayonet I still have was taken when Banks' men were routed. We called General Banks "good old Banks." He was in charge of the Commissary of General McDowell. Banks was deathly afraid of Jackson and his men, and whenever we were running short of food, ammunition, or other supplies we could get what we needed if "good old Banks" was close to us.

The battle of McDowell started early in May, 1862 [May 8, 1862]. General Milroy had apparently decided to make the battle a quick one. He threw all his forces against General [Edward] Johnson and when it got so Johnson could hardly hold the Yankee line[,] Jackson sent in parts of the Stonewall Brigade. Milroy's troops were forced back and he evacuated his positions at McDowell and retreated to Franklin. . . .

We whipped the Yankees at McDowell and ran them to Franklin. We then back-tracked to Bridgewater and from there to Harrisonburg, marching 25 to 30 miles per day. We then went to Front Royal where we whipped a part of Banks' army [May 23, 1862]. We then went to Kernstown and to Winchester where we whipped Banks' whole army [May 25, 1862], capturing about 1,100 prisoners, and ran him to Bolivar Heights which is on the west side of the Rappahannock River. The Maryland Heights prevented our crossing the river. We then went back to Cross Keys [June 8, 1862] where we whipped Fremont. We crossed the North River and the South River on bridges and whipped Shields. These battles took place on June 8 and 9, 1862. . . . We ran Shields down the River in this battle. It had taken Jackson about 40 days to clean

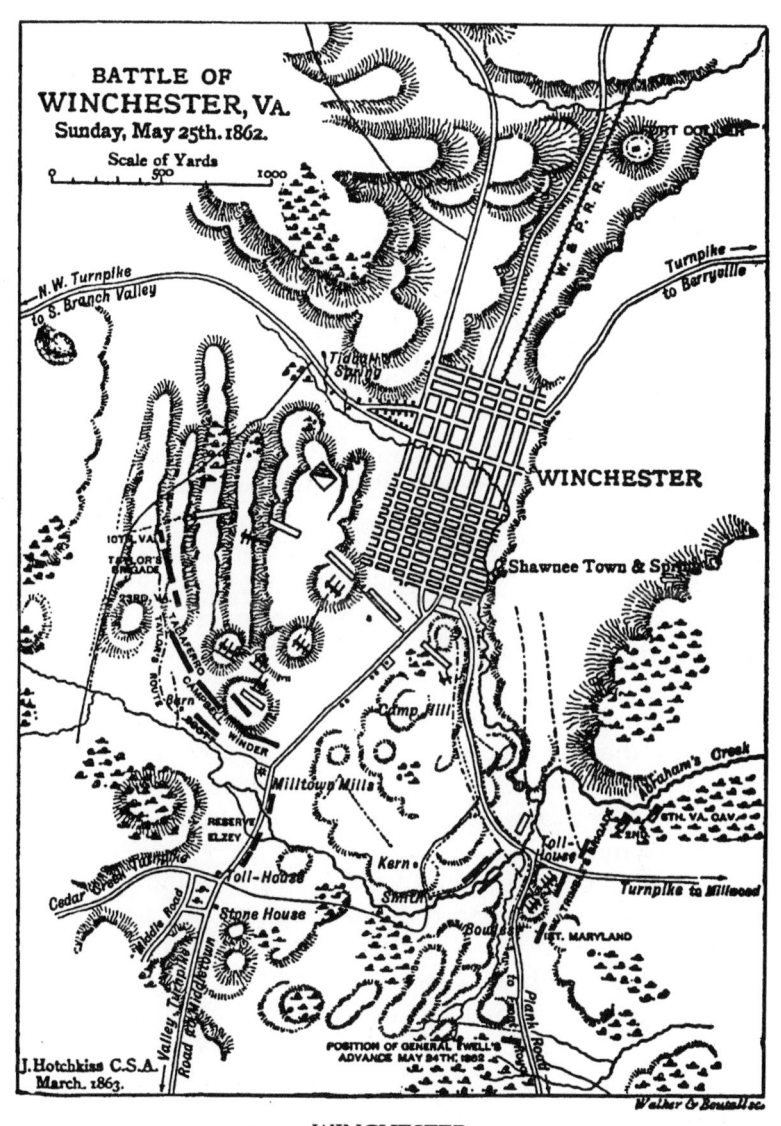

WINCHESTER

In October 1861 Jackson was commissioned a major general and sent to command the Valley district. In the course of the winter he drove the Federal troops from the district and went into winter quarters at Winchester. In March of 1862, Jackson began his famous Valley Campaign: Kernstown (March 23), McDowell (May 8), Front Royal (May 23), Winchester (May 25), Cross Keys (June 8), and Port Republic (June 9). Jackson defeated Union generals Shields, Milroy, Banks, and Fremont. This map was prepared by Jed Hotchkiss, Jackson's mapmaker (see lower left-hand corner of map).

up the Yankees in the Valley.

I used [the] "U.S." bayonet we captured from Banks (at McDowell) at Winchester, Port Republic, Mine Run and several other battles. Our men were not in the battle at Cross Keys. We were watching the movements of General Shields who was across the Rappahannock River.

I am not sure I had the bayonet on my [rifle] at the battle of Chancellorsville but believe I did. We never knew when Jackson would give the orders to "Set bayonets" or "Give them the bayonet." Whenever that order came the Yankees stopped or ran. Mine Run was followed by Briscoe Station where we again whipped the Yankees.

Jackson was completely a military man. I believe his war experience in Mexico, in a rolling country, was worth a lot to him. He knew Virginia and especially the Shenandoah Valley. He knew it better than any general on either side. I followed him when, more than once, he worked us around Banks, Hooker, and some of the other Yankee generals. He believed in speed and surprise. He had fought and worked with many of these generals and he knew their strong and weak points. Because of our loyalty to him we sometimes marched while asleep.

I remember on one march through a timbered section of the Valley we had to travel over a dusty road some two or three hundred yards in view of the Yankees. Jackson had us lengthen our lines and cut tree limbs and drag them behind us. The dust was so thick it hid us as we passed through the open space, and the longer time in passing gave the impression of a larger force than we had.

. . . Our clothes did wear out. Shoes were mighty hard to come by at times. When the ground was damp it was not so hard to march with a hole in the sole of the shoe, but on a road covered with rocks the going was rough. Sometimes we had to wrap our feet in old rags covering what had been a shoe. This was . . . necessary when the ground was frozen. ♦

THE HERO OF THE VALLEY
BY
WILLIAM H. ANDREWS
FIRST SERGEANT, COMPANY M
FIRST GEORGIA REGULARS

William H. Andrews joined the new state army raised upon Georgia's secession in January 1861. This state army was later incorporated into the Confederate Army as the First Georgia Regulars. This unit was not under Stonewall Jackson's command, but Sergeant Andrews saw General Jackson at Malvern Hill. He was 23 years old when he recorded the following in his diary.

About sunrise [on July 1, 1862, we were given] the command "Attention, First Brigade, take arms." The line was quickly formed, stacks of guns broken. . . . We moved in line of battle to the front. . . . We passed out of [a] field, then through a piece of woods, and entered another field, where we were halted.

While we were halted an officer was seen riding some 200 yards in front of us and going to our left. Such cheering I had never heard. The soldiers went wild as they tossed their caps in the air. The officer doffed his cap, spurred his horse, and was quickly out of sight. On asking who it was, I was told that it was Gen. T.J. Jackson, the hero of the valley. The first thing I looked at was his foot, having sometime before read in the newspaper where Gen. Jackson was the second man to mount the walls at Chapultepec, Mexico, and that his foot was 14 inches long. . . .

From what I saw of Gen. Jackson, he is a very ordinary looking man of medium size, his uniform badly soiled as though it had seen hard service. He wore a cap pulled down nearly to his nose. . . . He actually made a poor figure on horseback, with his stirrup leather six inches too short[,] putting his knees nearly level with his horse's back, and his heels turned out with his toes sticking behind his horse's foreshoulder. A sorry description of our most famous general, but a correct one. ♦

A. C. REDWOOD

BERDAN'S SHARPSHOOTERS
Battle of Malvern Hill, July 1, 1862

JACKSON AT CLOSE RANGE
BY
DAVID ELDRED HOLT
PRIVATE, COMPANY K
16TH MISSISSIPPI REGIMENT

David Holt was born November 27, 1843, in Woodville, Wilkinson County, Mississippi, the son of a prosperous doctor. At the beginning of the war he joined the Wilkinson Rifles, known later as Company K of the 16th Mississippi Regiment. Judged too young (at 17) by the Wilkinson Rifles to be accepted as a "full-fledged" soldier, David was made a "cadet," and was forced to stay at home until the fall of 1861, when, with his father's written consent, he was allowed to join the Rifles, then with Trimble's Brigade. In the spring of 1862, after taking part in driving the Union forces from Winchester, Private Holt saw General Jackson for the first time.

David Holt became a chemist after the war and worked for a drug company. He married, raised a family, and eventually moved to California where he became a minister. Late in life he moved to Florida where he wrote his memoirs of the war, which are called A MISSISSIPPI REBEL IN THE ARMY OF NORTHERN VIRGINIA. *He died there November 5, 1925.*

It was on the banks of the Potomac [May 1862] that I got my first view of General Jackson at close range. Our skirmish line was directly on the banks of the river, when the General and his staff rode up. They dismounted and earnestly looked across the river. We knew the General from the pictures we saw of him. Some of the boys remarked: "He is certainly up to scratch." He made brilliant moves, and we called him our "Old Jack," when we wanted to be particularly respectful and loving. ♦

THAT MAN JACKSON
BY
H.M. WHARTON
PRIVATE, GENERAL LEE'S ARMY

H.M. Wharton was only 12 years old when the Civil War began, but he managed to be in the breastworks below Petersburg--"a boy of sixteen"--in April 1865, "a soldier in an army of 40,000 men opposing fully five times that many on the other side." He was, however, still at home with his family in August 1862, after the Union defeat at Cedar Mountain, when he heard Federal troops speak of General Jackson, as he relates below.

Our family remained in the County of Culpepper [in Virginia] until the middle of the war. God took our dear mother from us; the older boys had to go to war and father was alone with his daughters and myself, I being the youngest child. As I was under age, and not large enough to be noticed, I was often in conversation with Federal officers, and also with those from the South. One army or the other seemed almost incessantly passing to and fro through our part of the State. It was my privilege to witness the battle of Cedar Mountain [August 9, 1862], which was fought two miles from my father's home, and the next day I rode over the field in company with him to see if we might, in any way, minister to the wants of the wounded and suffering. It was my first study of the battlefield, and the impression made upon my mind, when I saw hundreds of men lying in every position--the most of them dead, others wounded and dying--can never be removed.
. . .

I was standing in my father's yard when Pope's army commenced its retreat. Several stragglers came in to get a drink of water, and I inquired of them which way they were going. They answered, "Back where we came from." I asked them who was in command on the other side the day before. The reply was, "That man Jackson; his name is better than 10,000 men any day." Another conversation occurred . . . with reference to General Jackson. Several Federal officers who had been in the fight the day before were discussing whether General Jackson was a Christian. One said, "I do not believe he is a Christian, for if he was he would not be such a devil of a fighter"; the other said, "I do not know whether he is a Christian or not; but there is one thing for certain, if he ever makes up his mind to go to Heaven all hell can't keep him from it." Such was the impression that Stonewall Jackson had made upon the men of the Federal Army. ♦

&

> AND MEN SHALL TELL THEIR CHILDREN,
> THO' ALL OTHER MEMORIES FADE,
> THAT THEY FOUGHT WITH *STONEWALL JACKSON*
> IN THE OLD "STONEWALL BRIGADE"!
> --FROM THE *SONG OF THE REBEL*
> BY JOHN ESTEN COOKE

FOLLOW YOUR GENERAL, BOYS!
BY
CHARLES MINOR BLACKFORD

On August 16, 1862, Captain Blackford wrote to his wife in Lynchburg, Virginia, about the battle at "Slaughter Mountain," that is Cedar Mountain, which had taken place a week before, on August 9, 1862. Blackford begins these few paragraphs (from what is a very long letter) with a description of Confederate troops as they wait to draw up into line of battle. Then he tells of events in which General Stonewall Jackson plays only one of the central roles.

. . . [Here] I saw what I had never seen before--the men pinning strips of paper to their coats, with . . . name, company and regiment marked on them, so they could be identified if killed.

After standing at this point a long time, or what, at least, seemed to me a long time under the circumstances, the firing in my front and to the left of the road became very sharp and was nearing me rapidly, showing that our men had either been driven or were falling back. I could not see, because there were some low bushes and chapparel just in my front, but in an instant a regiment or two burst through into the open spot where I was standing, all out of order and mixed up with a great number of yankees. I could not understand it; I could not tell whether our men had captured the yankees or the yankees had broken through our line. In an instant, however, the doubt was put at rest, for General Jackson, with one or two of his staff, came dashing across the road from our right in great haste and excitement. As he got amongst the disordered troops he drew his sword and then reached over and took his battle-flag from my man, Bob Isbell, who was carrying it, and dropping his bridle-rein, waved it over his head, and at the same time cried out in a loud voice: "Rally, men! Remember Winder! Where's my Stonewall Brigade!! Forward men! Forward!!" As he did so he dashed to the front, and our men followed with a yell and drove everything before them. It was a wonderful scene--one which men do not often see. Jackson, usually, is an indifferent and slouchy-looking man, but then, with the "light of battle" shedding its radiance over him, his whole person was changed. His action as graceful as Lee's and his face was lit with the inspiration of heroism. The men would have followed him into the jaws of death itself; nothing could have stopped them, and nothing did. . . .

  Just as this wonderful scene was being enacted a very handsome and hatless yankee captain, not over twenty-one or two years of age, whose head was covered with clusters of really golden curls, and who had in his hand a broken sword, showing he had led the gallant charge which had broken our ranks, laid his hand on my knee as I sat on my horse and said, with great emotion, "What officer is that, Captain?" [A]nd when I told him . . . he seemed carried away with admiration, and, with that touch of nature that makes the whole world a-kin, he waved his broken sword around his head and shouted, "Hurrah for Stonewall Jackson! Follow your General, Boys!" I leaned over, almost with tears in my eyes and said, "You are too good a fellow for me to make a prisoner; take that path to the left and you can escape." He saluted . . . me with his broken sword, and disappeared in an instant. I hope he escaped. ♦

"STONEWALL JACKSON'S WAY."

BY

JOHN WILLIAMSON PALMER

This is the best known of the Civil War songs written in Stonewall Jackson's honor. For years after the war the identity of the author of the poem which provides the lyrics was in some doubt. It was actually written by John Williamson Palmer "within the sound of the firing at Antietam," in September 1862. Palmer was a Southern war correspondent for the NEW YORK TIMES *and the* NEW YORK TRIBUNE *who eventually joined the Confederate army as a combatant. Efforts to disguise the author and publisher of "Stonewall Jackson's Way" resulted in some inventive misidentifications. As late as 1904 an editor of a collection of poems and songs wrote that the verses were "found on a small piece of paper, all stained with blood, in [the] bosom of a dead soldier of the old Stonewall Brigade, after one of Jackson's battles in the Shenandoah Valley." The earliest published sheet music featuring the lyrics was printed in 1863 by J.W. Randolph of Richmond.*

Come, stack arms men, pile on the rails--
Stir up the campfire bright;
No matter if the canteen fails,
We'll make a roaring night.
Here Shenandoah crawls along,
Here burly Blue Ridge echoes strong,
To swell the brigade's rousing song,
Of "Stonewall Jackson's way."

We see him now--the old slouched hat
Couched o'er his eye askew--
The shrewd, dry smile--the speech so pat,
So calm, so blunt, so true,
The "Blue Light Elder" knows 'em well:
Says he, "That's Banks, he's fond of shell;
Lord, save his soul! we'll give him . . . " well
That's Stonewall Jackson's way.

Silence! ground arms! kneel all! caps off!
Old "Blue Light's" going to pray;
Strangle the fool that dares to scoff!
Attention! it's his way!
Appealing from his native sod,
"Hear us, Almighty God!
Lay bare thine arm, stretch forth thy rod,
Amen!" That's Stonewall Jackson's way.

He's in the saddle now! Fall in!
Steady! The whole brigade!
Hill's at the ford, cut off; we'll win
His way out, ball and blade.
What matter if our shoes are worn?
What matter if our feet are torn?
Quick step! we're with him ere the dawn!
That's Stonewall Jackson's way!

The sun's bright lances rout the mists
Of morning--and, by George!
Here's Longstreet, struggling in the lists,
Hemmed in an ugly gorge.
Pope and his Yankees, whipped before;
"Bayonets and grape!" hear Stonewall roar;
"Charge, Stuart! pay off Ashby's score,"
Is Stonewall Jackson's way!

Ah! maiden, wait, and watch, and yearn,
For news of Stonewall's band!
Ah! widow, read--with eyes that burn--
That ring upon thy hand!
Ah! wife, sew on, hope on, and pray!
Thy life shall not be all forlorn--
The foe had better ne'er been born,
That gets in Stonewall's way. ⌘

WITH JACKSON'S "FOOT CAVALRY" AT THE SECOND MANASSAS
BY
ALLEN CHRISTIAN REDWOOD

The following is an amalgamation of two of Redwood's articles, one from CENTURY MAGAZINE, *and the other (in italics below) from* SCRIBNER'S MONTHLY. *Redwood did much work for both these periodicals.*

In the operations of 1862, in Northern Virginia, the men of Jackson's corps have always claimed a peculiar proprietorship.... Some remnant of the old *esprit de corps* yet survives, and prompts this narrative.

❖

"Attention to orders!"

It was the evening dress-parade; in an old field beside the Charles City Road, a few miles from Richmond, the bayonets of a Confederate regiment were flashing back the last sunbeams of a midsummer day. But our "attention" now was something more than mere formality, as the curt tones of the adjutant proclaimed the order consigning us to the command of Stonewall Jackson.

The battle of the Seven Days was over. The last curl of the smoke which had rolled down the slopes of Malvern Hill had been borne away and dissipated, and the inevitable rain following the conflict had washed the air clean of all taint of its sulphurous burden. There were still to be seen, here and there in the woods, trees recently felled where no ax had been plied; there were acres --miles indeed--of country, now without a human inhabitant, where the soil was trodden like a highway; about the White House on the Pamunkey, fires were still smoldering among the debris of abandoned camps; here and there, in deserted farm-

houses, or else in some shady grove of timber near a spring, were field hospitals, in which some of the wounded yet lingered, awaiting transfer through convalescence, or the final discharge which death would confer; here and there, too, in out-of-the-way places in the woods, disfigured by dust and blood, and with faces blackened and swollen and distorted out of all likeness to the creator's image--prostrate in the underbrush, or standing upright and stark in mud and water as they had met their doom--were forms of gray or blue or brown clothing which betokened that they had been men. In Richmond, the tobacco factories and warehouses were so many hospitals and prisons, and full to overflowing with the city's late defenders or assailants, as the case might be; down the James, about Turkey Island Bend and the Westover plantation [near Harrison's Landing], the remnant of one army [i.e., the Union] was striving, under the protecting guns of its iron-clad fleet, to renew its shattered organization and impaired morale; while between it and the city, another army, in scarcely better plight, was laying to heart Napoleon's aphorism-- "After defeat, the saddest thing in war is victory."

  The opening of the attack which had rolled up McClellan's right flank had been [e]ntrusted to the raw troops of the newly organized "Light Division" of A.P. Hill. These brigades, and even many of the regiments composing them, had been but a short time associated together, were strangers to each other, and to the young major general, their commander, and thus the interdependence and homogeneity of feeling--such important elements of efficiency in modern warfare--were feeble or altogether wanting in the division. But these soldiers, in whose garments the smell of fire had not yet been found, were quick to learn the ways of war; the same men, who under the cannonade of the 26th of June--that ordeal always so trying to new troops--had suffered almost a panic, four days later stormed and captured those death-dealing guns with the steadiness and determination of veterans. Before the battle, they had scarcely

A. C. REDWOOD

CAPTURED BY JACKSON HIMSELF!

The following episode concerning General Jackson occurred during the Battle of Gaines' Mill (First Cold Harbor or The Chickahominy) on June 27, 1862, while Jackson was riding in advance of his skirmish-line with a few staff officers. The episode was told to D. H. Hill by Major T. O. Chestney:

"As Elzey's brigade was pressing forward to the line held by the Confederates . . . a squad of fifteen or twenty [Union] soldiers were [sic] encountered on their way to the rear. A tall fellow at the head of the little party drew special attention to himself by singing out to us at the top of his voice with an oath, 'Gentlemen, we had the honor of being captured by Stonewall Jackson himself,'—a statement which he repeated with evident pride all along the line, as our men tramped past. We subsequently learned that his story was true. General Jackson, having ridden some distance in advance, had come suddenly upon the blue-coats, and with his characteristic impetuosity had charged among them and ordered them to surrender, which they made haste to do."

known and cared even less to what division of the army they belonged; <u>now</u> if you asked one of them he would answer, with a perceptible pride in his mien and in his voice, that he was one of Hill's "Light Bobs."

For a while the mere relief from daily hardship and danger had been enjoyment in itself, but by degrees the dull routine of the camp grew more irksome than ever by contrast with the late stirring events; and in recounting the triumphs and glories of the battle, men lost sight of its attendant horrors, or saw them more and more dimly through the veil of retrospection. Dead comrades were buried out of sight, and so gradually they passed out of mind; the more seriously wounded were at home on leave, more to be envied than to be pitied, while the slightly wounded were returning to duty, physically or morally none the worse for their scratches.

And now we were going with Jackson! The very idea seemed to infuse a new spirit into the listless men, as if they felt already the refreshing breezes and tasted the cool springs of the far-off mountains. A month before, in our sultry squalid camps along the Chickahominy, the news had reached us of the brilliant Valley campaign, and in the midst of destitution and depression and doubt, with the enemy at the very gates of the capital, the bulletins of McDowell, Front Royal, Winchester, Cross Keys, Port Republic, read like a fairy tale: the contrast with our own tedious inaction lent a charm to the record of these stirring events, while scurvied mouths watered, and stomachs nauseated with eternal ration-bacon fairly yearned for the tents of Israel filled with blockade dainties, and for the teeming wagons of "Commissary" General Banks. With feverish interest we devoured the accounts of rapid marches, of sudden appearances where least expected, which had frustrated every combination of the enemy and conferred upon the troops of the mountain department the anomalous sobriquet of "Foot Cavalry."

The commander who was thus harvesting laurels daily--

A. C. REDWOOD

JOINING JACKSON'S CORPS
"The very idea seemed to infuse a new spirit into the listless men...."
– *ALLEN CHRISTIAN REDWOOD*

the first crop that season had borne, after long and sorrowful sowing, upon Confederate soil--had been, only a year ago, an obscure, plodding professor of natural philosophy at the Virginia Military Institute; remarkable chiefly for certain eccentricities of manner, and something of a butt for the witticisms of the thoughtless young cadets, because of what they regarded as too rigid exactness in his enforcement of the regulations. . . .

❖

. . . The awkward martinet professor, described by some of our number who had been students in his classes at Lexington, did not fill the measure of the central figure of the Valley campaign; our minds would not be content with dry statistics; their familiar "Old Jack" was not like our "Stonewall." The masses of his countrymen found something peculiarly acceptable in the character of the man, apart from his services: his retiring modesty, his indifference to display, his simple trust in the Giver of all victory, were shining virtues in the eyes of the people who had only taken up arms in behalf of what they considered their dearest rights, and with no care for the pomp and circumstance of war.

His very homeliness was a recommendation to the essentially practical-minded Southerner, regarding himself as the peer of any man, and constitutionally intolerant of the pretension symbolized in gold-lace and other fripperies of official rank. To such a one the old faded gray coat and cap of the Valley campaign were emblematic of something after his own heart. In a contest which, in the estimation of the participants on either side, partook the nature of a crusade, the man whose first care, after the "fatiguing day" upon which he himself had shed most glory, was to forward his subscription to a Sunday school at home; the man whose negro servant claimed to foretell a battle by the omen that his master rose frequently during the night to pray--this man would clearly "do to tie to." A hundred stories illustrative of these traits had already gathered about his name and invested him who bore it with a mysterious interest, and while they served to draw him home to our hearts, as a representative man, not by any fortuitous combination of chances, but because of that inherent fitness which the chances of war had brought to light. This prestige attached also in some degree to the troops whom he had unfailingly led to victory, and whom we as yet scarcely conceived as mortal men in all the ways like unto ourselves.

But our "attention" now was something more than mere formality, as the curt tones of the adjutant proclaimed the order consigning us to the command of Stonewall Jackson.

❖

After the check to Pope's advance at Cedar Mountain, on the 9th of August, and while we awaited the arrival of Longstreet's troops, A. P. Hill's division rested in camp at Crenshaw's Farm. Our brigade (Field's) was rather a new one in organization and experience, most of us having "smelt powder" for the first time in the Seven Days before Richmond. We got on the field at Cedar Mountain too late to be more than slightly engaged, but on the 10th and 11th covered the leisurely retreat to Orange Court House without molestation. When about a week later Pope began to retreat in the direction of the Rappahannock, we did some sharp marching through Stevensburg [*sometimes written "Stephensby"*] and Brandy Station, but did not come up with him until he was over the river. While our artillery was duelling with him across the stream, I passed the time with my head in the scant shade of a sassafras

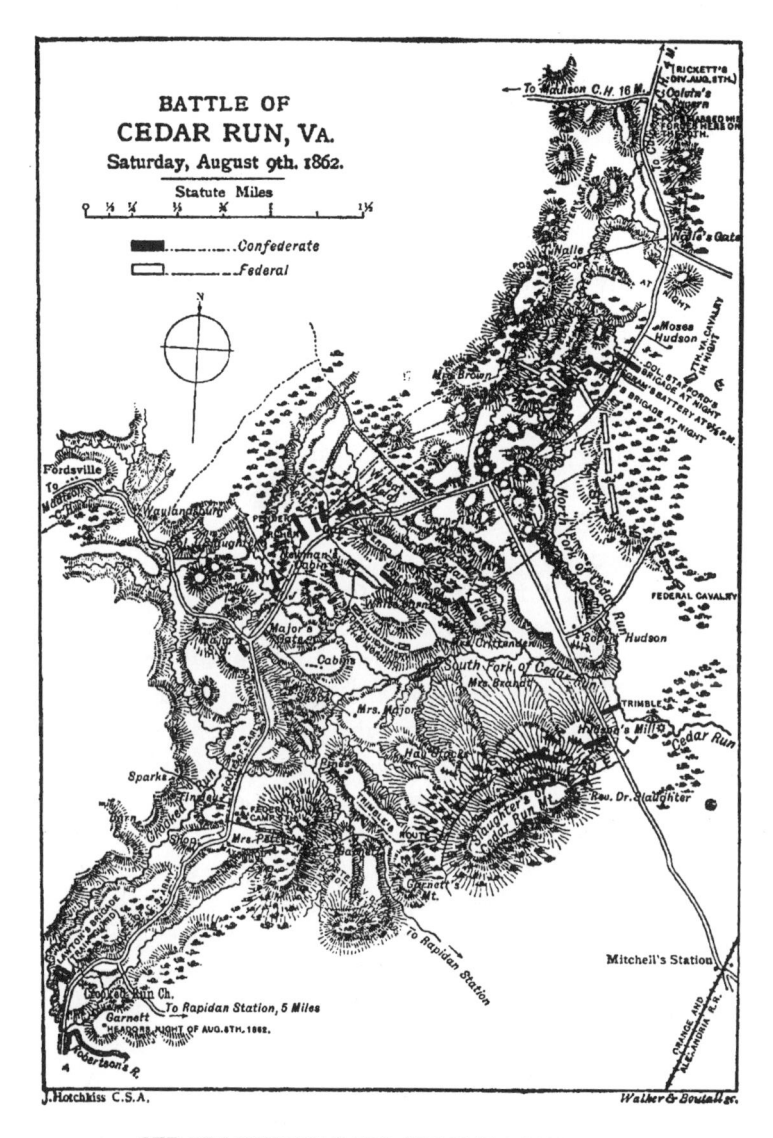

CEDAR MOUNTAIN TO SECOND MANASSAS

Jackson took part in the operations against McClellan, and in July of 1862 he was again detached and sent to Gordonsville to look after his old enemies from the Valley, who were gathering under Pope. He was now a lieutenant general commanding the Second Corps. On August 9th he crossed the Rapidan and defeated Banks at Cedar Mountain (Cedar Run). On August 25th he passed around Pope's right flank, forcing Pope to let go his hold upon the Rappahannock. The armies met at Second Manassas (Second Bull Run), and with stubborn fighting Jackson held his own until Longstreet could come up. Finally, Pope was routed on August 29 and 30 of 1862.

bush by the roadside, with a chill and fever brought from the Chickahominy low-grounds. In the latter connection, I improved the shining hours by [writing] a pathetic request in my notebook, to whom it might concern, that my body might be decently buried.

For the next few days there was skirmishing at the fords, we moving up the south bank of the river, the enemy confronting us on the opposite side. The weather was very sultry, and the troops much weakened by disorders induced by their diet of unsalted beef, eked out with green corn and unripe apples; as a consequence there was a good deal of straggling. I got behind several times, but managed to catch up from day to day. Once some cavalry made a dash across the river at our train; I joined a party in arrears like myself, and we fought them off on our own hook until Trimble's brigade, the rear guard, came up.

We were then opposite the Warrenton Springs, and were making a great show of crossing, Early's brigade having been thrown over the river and somewhat smartly engaged. I have since heard that [General Jubal Early] remonstrated more than once at the service required of him, receiving each time in reply a peremptory order from Jackson "to hold his position." He finally retorted: "Oh! well, old Jube can *die*, if *that's* what he wants, but tell General Jackson I'll be _____ if this position *can* be held!"

The brigade moved off next morning, leaving me in the grip of my ague [*chills, fever, and sweats*], which reported promptly for duty, and, thanks to a soaking over night, got in its work most effectually. The fever did not let go until about sundown, when I made two feeble trips to carry my effects about one hundred yards to the porch of a house close by, where I passed the night without a blanket--mine having been stolen between the trips. I found a better one next morning thrown away in a field,

A. C. REDWOOD

SHORT RATIONS

"Apples and corn, corn and apples, were our only fare. We ate them raw, roasted, boiled together, and fried. They served to sustain life, and that was all.

"I have often been asked about the 'Rebel Yell.' I have always answered that the Rebs were savage with hunger, and men always 'holler' when hungry."

– *ALEXANDER HUNTER*

A. C. REDWOOD

SINEWS OF WAR
"Two ribs on a stump were indicated as my share, and I broiled them on the coals. . . ."

— *ALLEN CHRISTIAN REDWOOD*

and soon after came up with the command in bivouac, and breakfasting on some beef which had just been issued. Two ribs on a stump were indicated as my share, and I broiled them on the coals and made the first substantial meal for forty-eight hours. This was interrupted by artillery fire from beyond the river, and as I was taking my place in line, my colonel, whom I knew rather personally, considering our relative rank, ordered me to the ambulance to recruit. Here I got a dose of Fowler's solution, "in lieu of quinine," and at the wagon-camp fared better than for a long time before. Meanwhile, they were having a hot time down at the Waterloo bridge, which the enemy's engineers were trying to burn, while some companies of sharpshooters under Lieutenant Robert Healey of "ours"--whose rank was no measure of his services or merit--were disputing the attempt. A concentrated fire from the Federal batteries failed to dislodge the plucky riflemen, while our guns were now brought up, and some hard pounding ensued. But at sunset the bridge still stood, and I "spread down" for the night under the pole of a wagon, fully expecting a serious fight on the morrow.

I was roused by a courier's horse stepping on my leg, and found this rude waking meant orders to move. With no idea whither, we pulled out at half-past two in the morning, and for some time traveled by fields and "new cuts" in the woods, following no road, but by the growing dawn evidently keeping up the river. Now Hill's "Light Division" was to earn its name, and qualify itself for membership in Jackson's corps. The hot August sun rose up, clouds of choking dust enveloped the hurrying column, but on and on the march was pushed without relenting. Knapsacks had been left behind in the wagons, and haversacks were empty by noon; for the unsalted beef spoiled and was thrown away, and the column subsisted itself, without process of commissariat, upon green corn and apples from the fields and orchards along the route, devoured while marching; for there were no stated meal-times and no systematic halts for rest. It was far on in the night when the column stopped, and the weary men dropped beside their stacked muskets and were instantly asleep, without so much as unrolling a blanket. A few hours of much-needed repose, and they were shaken up again long before "crack of day," and limped on in the darkness, only half awake. There was no mood for speech, nor breath to spare if there had been--only the shuffling tramp of the marching feet, the steady rumbling of wheels, the creak and rattle and clank of harness and accouterment, with an occasional order, uttered under the breath and always the same: "Close up! close up, men!"

❖

Whither were we going in such haste? No one could guess, unless it was, perhaps, he who was now seen frequently riding back and forth along the toiling column, and who by degrees had come to be recognized as its guiding spirit--Jackson. It would have been easy to have mistaken him for the courier of one of his brigadiers, for all external tokens to the contrary; his single-breasted coat of rusty gray, sun-scorched about the shoulders until it was almost yellow, and his plain cadet-cap of the same hue, tilted forward until the visor rested almost upon his nose, were meaner in appearance than the make-up of many a smart fellow in the ranks whose musket was the badge of his station; and not a quartermaster in the corps but would have considered Jackson's gaunt old sorrel a bad swap for his own nag. But the eager look in his eyes when one could catch a glimpse of them under the cap-brim, the firm set of his lips and the impatient jerking of his arm from time to time, were all signs by which we were to learn to know that "something was up," though we could not read them then.

❖

All this time we had the vaguest notions as to our objective: at first we had expected to strike the enemy's flank, but as the march prolonged itself, a theory obtained that we were going to the Valley. But we threaded Thoroughfare Gap, heading eastward, and in the morning of the third day (Aug. 27) struck a railroad running north and south--Pope's "line of communication and supply." Manassas was ours!

❖

... Ah! General Pope, better had you looked a little more carefully to your "lines of communication and supply." The longest way around is sometimes the nearest way home, and "disaster and shame now lurk in the rear" indeed--for Stonewall Jackson has flanked you!

❖

What a prize it was! Here were long warehouses full of stores; cars loaded with boxes of new clothing *en route* to General Pope, but destined to adorn the "backs of his enemies"; camps, sutlers' shops--"no eating up" of good things. In view of the abundance, it was no easy matter to determine what we should eat and drink and wherewithal we should be clothed; one was limited in his choice to only so much as he could personally transport, and the one thing needful in each individual case was not always

A. C. REDWOOD
"WHAT A PRIZE IT WAS!"
"Here were long warehouses full of stores; cars loaded with boxes of new clothing.... In view of the abundance, it was no easy matter to determine what we should eat and drink...."
– ALLEN CHRISTIAN REDWOOD

readily found. However, as the day wore on, an equitable distribution of our wealth was effected by barter, upon a crude and irregular tariff in which the rule of supply and demand was somewhat complicated by fluctuating estimates of the imminence of marching orders. A mounted man would offer large odds in shirts or blankets for a pair of spurs or a bridle; and while in anxious quest of a pair of shoes I fell heir to a case of cavalry half-boots, which I would gladly have exchanged for the object of my search. For a change of underclothing and a pot of French mustard I owe grateful thanks to the major of the Twelfth Pennsylvania Cavalry, with regrets that I could not use his library. Whisky was, of course, at a high premium, but a keg of "lager"--a drink far less popular then than now--went begging in our company.

A. C. REDWOOD

JACKSON'S FOOT CAVALRY

"Such specters of men they were—gaunt-cheeked and hollow-eyed, hair, beard, clothing, and accouterments covered with dust—only their faces and hands, where mingled soil and sweat streaked and crusted the skin, showing any departure from the whitey-gray uniformity."

– ALLEN CHRISTIAN REDWOOD

But our brief holiday was drawing to a close, for by this time General Pope had some inkling of the disaster which lurked in his rear. When, some time after dark, having set fire to the remnant of the stores, we took the road to Centreville, our mystification as to Jackson's plans was complete. Could he actually be moving on Washington with his small force, or was he seeking escape to the mountains? The glare of our big bonfire lighted up the country for miles, and was just dying out when we reached Centreville. The corduroy road had been full of pitfalls and stumbling-blocks, to some one of which our cracked axle had succumbed before we crossed Bull Run, and being on ahead, I did not know of the casualty until it was too late to save my personal belongings involved in the wreck. Thus suddenly reduced from affluence to poverty, just as the gray dawn revealed the features of the forlorn little hamlet, typical of this war-harried region, I had a distinct sense of being a long way from home. The night's march had seemed to put the climax to the endurance of the jaded troops. Such specters of men they were--gaunt-cheeked and hollow-eyed, hair, beard, clothing, and accouterments covered with dust--only their faces and hands where mingled soil and sweat streaked and crusted the skin, showing any departure from the whitey-gray uniformity. The ranks were sadly thinned, too, by the stupendous work of the last week. Our regiment, which had begun the campaign 1,015 strong and had carried into action at Richmond 620, counted off that Thursday morning (Aug. 28) just 82 muskets! Such were the troops about to deliver battle on the already historic field of Manassas.

 We were soon on the road again, heading west; we crossed Stone Bridge, and a short distance beyond, our ambulances halted, the brigade having entered some woods on the right of the road ahead--going into camp, I thought.

This pleasing delusion was soon dispelled by artillery firing in front, and our train was moved off through the fields to the right, out of range, and parked near Sudley Church. Everything pointed to a battle next day; the customary hospital preparations were made, but few, if any, wounded came in that night, and I slept soundly, a thing to be grateful for. My bedfellow and I had decided to report for duty in the morning, knowing that every musket would be needed. I had picked up a good "Enfield" with the proper trappings, on the road from Centreville, to replace my own left in the abandoned ambulance; and having broken my chills, and gained strength from marching unencumbered, was fit for service--as much so as were the rest at least.

    Friday morning early, we started in what we supposed to be the right direction, guided by the firing, which more and more betokened that the fight was on. Once we stopped for a few moments at a field hospital to make inquiries, and were informed that our brigade was farther along to the right. General Ewell was carried by on a stretcher while we were there, having lost his leg the evening before. Very soon we heard sharp musketry over a low ridge which we had been skirting, and almost immediately we became involved with stragglers from that direction--Georgians, I think they were. It looked as if a whole line was giving way, and we hurried on to gain our own colors before it should grow too hot. The proverbial effect of bad company was soon apparent. We were halted by a Louisiana major, who was trying to rally these fragments upon his own command. My companion took the short cut out of the scrape by showing his "sick permit," and was allowed to pass; mine, alas! was in my cartridge-box with my other belongings in that unlucky ambulance. The major was courteous but firm; listened to my story with more attention than I could have expected, but attached my person all the same. "Better stay with us, my boy, and if you do your duty I'll make it right with your company officers when the fight's over. They won't find fault with you when they know you've been in with the 'Pelicans,'" he added, as he assigned me to company "F."

The command was as unlike my own as it is possible to conceive. Such a congress of nations only the cosmopolitan Crescent City could have sent forth, and the tongues of Babel seemed resurrected in its speech; English, German, French, and Spanish, all were represented, to say nothing of Doric brogue and local "gumbo," and its voluble exercise was set off by a vehemence of utterance and gesture curiously at variance with the reticence of our Virginians. On the

A. C. REDWOOD

A LOUISIANA PELICAN

"They won't find fault with you when they know you've been in with the 'Pelicans' . . ."

– ALLEN CHRISTIAN REDWOOD

whole, I did not take to my comrades very kindly, and cordially consigned Company "F" to a region even more redolent of sulphur than the scene of our enforced connection. In point of fact, we burned little powder that day, and my promised distinction as a "Pelican" [for the time being] was cheaply earned.

The battalion did a good deal of counter-marching and some skirmishing, but most of the time we were acting as support to a section of Cutshaw's battery. The tedium of this last service my companions relieved by games of "seven up," with a greasy, well-thumbed deck, and in smoking cigarettes, rolled with great dexterity between the deals. Once, when a detail was ordered to go some distance under fire to fill the canteens of the company, a hand was dealt to determine who should go, and the decision was accepted by the loser without demur. Our numerous shifts of position completely confused what vague ideas I had of the situation, but we must have been near our extreme left at Sudley Church, and never very far from my own brigade, which was warmly engaged that day and the day following. Towards evening we were again within sight of Sudley Church. I could see the light of fires among the trees as if cooking for the wounded was going on, and the idea occurred to me that there I could easily learn the exact position of my proper people. Once clear of my major and his polyglot "Pelicans," the rest would be plain sailing.

My flank movement was easily effected, and I suddenly found myself the *most* private soldier on that field; there seemed to be nobody else anywhere near. I passed a farmhouse which seemed to have been used as a hospital, and where I picked up a Zouave fez. Some cavalrymen were there, one of whom advised me not to "go down there," but as he gave no special reason and did not urge his views, I paid no heed to him, but went on my way down a long barren slope, ending at a small watercourse at the bottom, beyond which the ground rose abruptly and was covered by small growth. The deepening twilight and strange solitude about me, with the remembrance of what had happened a year ago on this same ground, made me feel uncomfortably lonely. By this time I was close to the stream, and while noting the lay of the land on the opposite bank with regard to choice of a crossing place, I became aware of a man observing me from the end of the cut above. I could not distinguish the color of his uniform, but the crown of his hat tapered suspiciously, I thought, and instinctively I dropped the butt of my rifle to the ground and reached behind me for a cartridge.

"Come here!" he called--his accent was worse than his hat.

"Who are you?" I responded as I executed the movement of "tear cartridge."

He laughed and said something--evidently not to me--then invited me to "come and see." Meanwhile I was trying to draw my rammer, but this operation was arrested by the dry click of several gunlocks, and I found myself covered by half a dozen rifles, and my friend of the steeple-crown, with less urbanity in his intonation, called out to me to "drop that." In our brief intercourse he had acquired a curious influence over me. I did so.

My captors were of Kearny's division, on picket. They told me they thought I was deserting until they saw me try to load. I could not account for their being where they were, and when they informed me that they had Jackson surrounded and that he must surrender next day, though I openly [scorned] the notion, I must own the weight of evidence seemed to be with them. The discussion of this and kindred topics was continued until a late hour that night with the sergeant of the guard at Kearny's headquarters, where I supped in unwonted luxury on hardtack and "genuine" coffee, the sergeant explaining that the fare was no better because of our destruction of their supplies at the Junction. Kearny's orderly gave me a blanket, and so I passed the night. We were astir in the morning (Aug. 30), and I saw Kearny as he passed with his staff to the front--a spare, erect, military figure, looking every inch the fighter he was--but with the shadow of his doom hovering over him even then. He fell three days later, killed by some of my own brigade.

Near Stone Bridge I found about 500 other prisoners, mostly stragglers picked up along the line of our march. Here my polite provost-sergeant turned me over, and after drawing rations--hard-tack, and coffee and sugar mixed--we took the road to Centreville, having to stand a good deal of chaff on the way at our forlorn appearance, for that thoroughfare was thronged with troops, trains, and batteries. We were a motley crowd enough, certainly, and it *did* look as if our friends in blue were having their return innings. More than once that day as I thought of our thin line back yonder, I wondered how the boys were making it, for disturbing rumors came to us as we lay in a field near Centreville, exchanging rude [banter] across the cordon of sentries surrounding us. We received recruits from time to time who brought the same unvarying story, "Jackson hard pressed--no news of Longstreet yet." (He was there, but keeping silent.) So the day wore on. Towards evening there was a noticeable stir in the camps around us, much riding to and fro of couriers and orderlies, and now we thought we could hear more distinctly the deep-toned, jarring growl which had interjected itself at intervals all the afternoon through the trivial buzz about us. Watchful of indications, we noted too that the drift of wagons and ambulances was *from* the battlefield, and soon orders came for us to take the road in the same direction. The cannonading down the pike was sensibly nearer now, and at times we could catch even the roll of muskets, and once we thought we could distinguish, faint and far off, murmurous modulation of sound familiar to our ears as the charging shout of the gray people--but this may have been fancy. All the same, we gave tongue to the cry, and shouts of "Longstreet! Longstreet's at 'em, boys! Hurrah for Longstreet!" went up from the column, while the guards trudged beside us in sulky silence.

There is not much more to tell. An all-day march on Sunday through rain and mud brought us to Alexandria, where we were locked up for the night in a cotton factory. Monday we embarked on a transport steamer, and the next evening were off at Fort Monroe, where we got news of Pope's defeat. I was paroled and back in Richmond within ten days of my capture, and then and there learned how completely Jackson had eclipsed his former fame on his baptismal battlefield.

❖

Space forbids more than a passing mention of the succeeding events of that memorable campaign. The world knows the story of Jackson's grim fight to hold his ground, while Pope, McClellan, and Burnside were closing in upon him, and his own lagging succor held off; of that sharp, short skirmish in the blinding rain at Chantilly where brave Phil Kearney fell in front of our brigade.

The bright bracing October days [came]. Since the return from Maryland there had been no very active hostilities and the troops were resting in their camps. . . . Like other people in prosperous circumstances, we came gradually to be quite fastidious in our consideration of camping places, and in view of the abundance of fine timber which surrounded us and the bold springs which gushed from every hillside, were luxuriously extravagant in the matter of fuel--if, indeed, generous fires might not be reckoned among the necessaries of life, now that the nights were becoming frosty, while as yet we had but . . . scanty [summer clothing] for all defense against the nipping air. Few companies could parade a sound pair of trousers; an overcoat was a distinctive badge of high official rank, and tents had long since passed among things of tradition. The . . . [troops] were like a mob of schoolboys in their excess of animal spirits, which, deprived of outlet through the channels of hard fighting and marching, found vent in noisy hilarity upon the least provocation; for now that the wagons were up and "pone" bread and beef stews reappeared on the menu, the Foot Cavalry, feeling its keep, waxed fat and kicked. Two causes were potent above all others for the calling forth of this vociferous demonstration--the chase of a hare or the appearance of Jackson near the camps. His dislike of notoriety was well known, and he never failed to avoid it when it was possible; for this very reason, the men who, when General Lee passed, were wont to stand silent by the roadside and with heads reverently uncovered, would yell like demons for the sake of "making old Jack run," and all the camps would turn out in force at the signal.

It was the end of a bleak November day; the fires of railway ties, extending in a long line either way as far as the eye could follow, made still more neutral by contrast with their ruddy light the dun-gray fields of stubble, and the woods in which the gorgeous panoply of the earlier season was paling into russet and ashy tones. The work was over and we were waiting with some impatience for the order to take up the line of march back to camp; for the evening air struck chilly through our threadbare and tattered jackets, and we had eaten nothing since early morning. Moreover, a wild rumor had spread abroad that an issue of fresh pork awaited our return, and though the long habit of expecting nothing good until it came secured us against any serious disappointment, there were not wanting tender memories of "short" biscuit to raise out anticipations higher than we cared to own.

Thus preoccupied, we are fain to refer to a distant cheering further down the line to tidings of the coming rations, and we gather by the roadside in order to get off the more promptly when our turn shall arrive. The sound grows more and more distinct every moment, and now, far down the road some moving object can just be discerned in a cloud of dust which travels rapidly our way. Nearer and nearer it comes; louder and more enthusiastic ring the shouts, and now we make out in the dust a figure of a single horseman, with a clump of others trailing off into obscurity behind him--Jackson is coming! A moment more, and he is here, going at almost top speed; his hat is off; his hair blown back from his broad white forehead; his eyes dancing and his cheeks aglow with excitement, and the rush of keen air.

And now the cheers grow deafening and ragged hats are swung more wildly still as the men of the Foot Cavalry recognize their leader. The cavalcade in the dust up the road, cheered to the very last lagging courier of the escort--for we are in good humor now with ourselves and the world. And as we step briskly out upon our homeward march, the air feels fresh and invigorating, and the miles seem shorter than they were in the morning; even the beloved biscuit is of minor consequence, and the promised pork pales beside the thought which fills us--that we have seen Jackson! ♦

A. C. REDWOOD

"JACKSON IS COMING!"

"He has a first rate face, and seems a plainly dressed Captain of the Cavalry.... His uniform is fine enough, certainly, for the life he leads. But the imagination is piqued, you know, by the absence of pretension.... Stonewall don't like to come about the army much. The boys keep him bareheaded all the time. When they begin to cheer he usually pulls off his hat, spurs his fine horse, and runs through, greeted with cheers every step for five miles."

– *A MAN IN THE RANKS*

JACKSON OR A RABBIT
BY
BERRY GREENWOOD BENSON
PRIVATE IN STONEWALL JACKSON'S "FOOT CAVALRY"
AND LATER SERGEANT,
SHARPSHOOTER, AND CONFEDERATE SCOUT
IN THE BATTALION OF SHARPSHOOTERS
OF THE FIRST SOUTH CAROLINA REGIMENT

Berry Benson was born February 9, 1843, in Hamburg, South Carolina. He was one month short of being 18 when he joined a local militia which was officially mustered into service on January 8, 1861--months before the firing on Fort Sumter which began the Civil War. Benson enlisted as a private, but as a scout and sharpshooter he rose "quickly to the rank of sergeant." He was captured twice, and although he fought from First Manassas to Appomattox, he never surrendered. He simply went home, still carrying his precious rifle.

Berry Benson lived to be 80 years old, having had "a happy life as a family man." His figure graces the top of the Confederate monument on Broad Street in Augusta, Georgia, the hometown of the woman he married (Jennie Oliver) and right across the Savannah River from his own hometown of Hamburg, South Carolina.

Of the times I have heard [Jackson] cheered, I will tell of two. It was just after the battle of Sharpsburg [September 16, 1862]. Having crossed back into Virginia, we were marched to the B. & O.R.R., which we burnt for a long distance, destroying the telegraph also, cutting down the posts and tangling up the wires. We had torn up the road and burnt it and were marching back. Stopping to rest in the woods, we stacked arms just on the side of the road and lay down.

While lying here, we heard a faint yell in the distance, back on the road. The men began to say: "Jackson or a rabbit; Jackson or a rabbit."

The yell continuing and growing louder and nearer, everybody says, "It's Jackson! It's Jackson!"

Directly came the sound of horse's feet galloping.

COURTESY SHORNE HARRISON

CONFEDERATE MEMORIAL IN AUGUSTA, GEORGIA

Berry Benson's figure in stone is perched high above Augusta, Georgia. Robert E. Lee's figure is at the base, bottom, left, and Stonewall Jackson's is at bottom, right. T.R.R. Cobb's and W.H.T. Walker's are on the opposite corners of the base, in back.

Then as all men rose, waving hats in the air and cheering the rider, came Jackson at a furious gallop, looking neither to the right nor to the left, not even paying the least heed to a stand of arms belonging to my company that stood in the road, but riding over them, scattering them right and left. After him, some fifty yards behind[,] came his aides, trying to keep him in sight. I have often thought that of all the relics of the war, I would rather have the gun that his horse's hoof struck than any other.

"Jackson or a rabbit!" That was the cry always made when a distant yell was heard, for whether one or the other, no pair of eyes would ever rest on him, but the mouth under them opened and gave vent to a prolonged yell. They were both cheered the same, only Jackson with "hats off."

The other time I speak of was at Harper's Ferry [September 1862]. We were all occupied with one thing or another, just after the surrender [of Union troops], the prisoners moving freely amongst us, though well guarded, when the cry was heard and the clattering hoofs.

"What's the matter?" asked the prisoners.

"Jackson's coming!" was the answer.

All feet rushed to the road, and such a cheer as was set up by men in grey and men in blue has seldom been heard. For the prisoners all cheered him just as lustily and heartily as we did ourselves. And we felt very kindly toward them for it. ♦

UNCLE STONE WALL
BY
JAMES THOMPSON
PRIVATE, COMPANY H
11TH GEORGIA REGIMENT

In the course of his life, General Thomas Jonathan Jackson was given many nicknames. His classmates at West Point called him "Old Jack" and "The General," and when he taught at the Virginia Military Institute the cadets called him "Hick," "Old Hickory" (these two harking back to President Andrew Jackson), "Square Box" (a reference to his large feet) and "Tom Fool" (a reference to his eccentricities, which the boys found foolish). Later, during the war, the troops also gave him nicknames. There was, of course, the famous "Stonewall," but his own men preferred the by then familiar "Old Jack," another version of this being "Old Jax." Other names given him were "Old Blue Light" ("Elder Blue Light" being a variation with a reference to his religious zeal and both referring, presumably, to his blue eyes and the way they were said to light up in battle), "Lemon Sucker," "Mountain Fox," and "The Wagon Hunter" (because he sought and captured the enemy's commissary wagons).

Private James Thompson, from Walton County, Georgia, wrote the following letter to a soldier friend on October 1, 1862, following the Battle of Sharpsburg (Antietam), in which he confers on his beloved commander his own affectionate sobriquet. A few days later, on October 5, Thompson wrote to his friend again: "You wanted to know if i was under stone wall or not. I am. He is a sorry looking chance...." The following month Private Thompson died of smallpox.

Wee just whiped them out completely hear. When wee fell back out of Md. across the river "Uncle Stone Wall" lay s[t]ill untill the Yankies all got over on this side then he picked into them and just slaughtered them and while thay were wading the river trying to Get back to Meriland ... wee runn Artilry upon the bank & Throwed Grape shot and canister among them, so the river was completely damed up so thick with blood that the river looked like blood for miles below.... You can tell the boys that they may brag on John Morgan, but he cant come up with "Uncle Stone." Tell them he dont Get behind stumps & trees as thay say thay did. We hant got the trees & stumps to Get behind. They say he is like a flee. When thay think thay have got him fast & go in to get him out, he is clear Gone & is whipping them somewhir elce. Some of the boys swares 'Stone Wall' can kick up the devil in 5 minuts time. It dose look like he can hav a fight just when he Gets ready.

You say Morgan is taring up Kentucki. I think he is wrong for destroying the country. When wee went into Meriland wee didnt burn a pear of rails or pull a apple or rosineer [*roasting ear*] without leaf [*permission*] from the oaner. Wee were in 2 1/2 miles of the Pencilvania line, rite among the Unionest. Wee dident say anything out of the way to anybody. ♦

A. C. REDWOOD

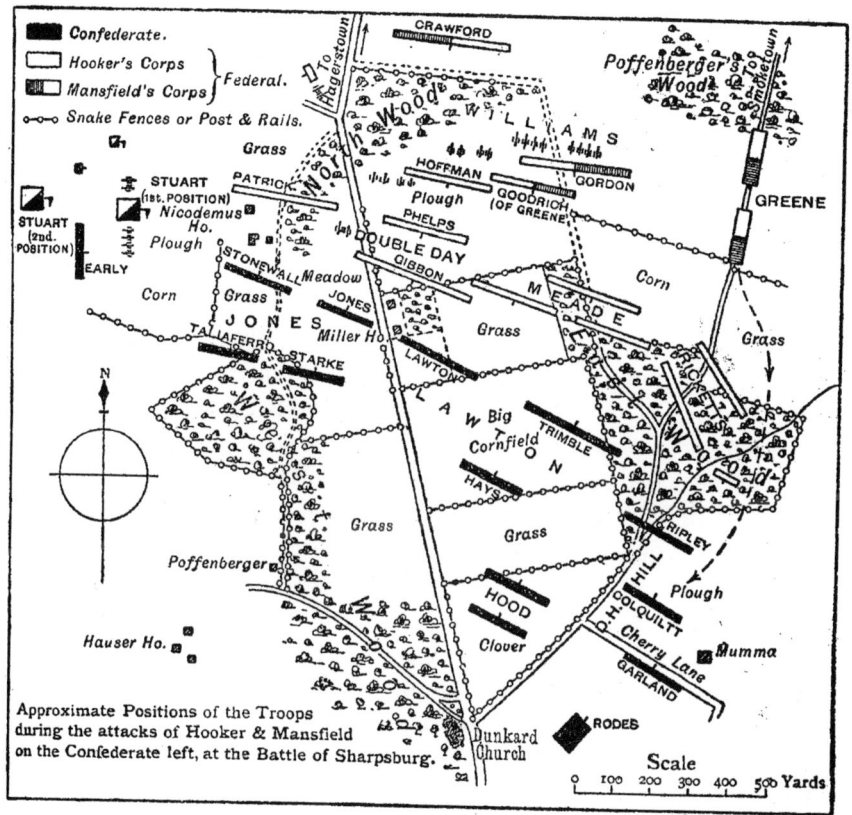

THE MARYLAND CAMPAIGN

At the beginning of the Maryland Campaign, Jackson captured Harper's Ferry along with 11,000 prisoners, 72 guns, and a large cache of arms. Then by a forced march reached Sharpsburg (Antietam) on September 16th where, starting the next morning, he commanded the left wing of the Confederate Army. In the war's singlest bloody day, he replused with his thin line the corps of Hooker, Mansfield, and Sumner which were in succession hurled against him. Later in the day, A. P. Hill's division of Jackson's Corps which had been left at Harper's Ferry, reached the field just in time to defeat Burnside on the right.

JACKSON'S RAGGED REBELS

This passage, apparently written to a Northern newspaper by a Union soldier who had become a prisoner of the Confederates, describes the condition of Jackson's army at the close of the second year of the Civil War, after the defeat of the Union army at Fredericksburg.

We had men enough, well enough equipped and well enough posted, to have devoured the ragged, imperfectly armed and equipped host of our enemies from off the face of the earth. Their artillery horses are poor, starved frames of beasts, tied on to their carriages and caissons with odds and ends of rope and strips of raw hide. Their supply and ammunition trains look like a congregation of all the crippled California emigrant trains that ever escaped off the desert out of the clutches of the rampaging Indians. The men are ill-dressed, ill-equipped, and ill-provided--a set of ragamuffins that a man is ashamed to be seen among, even when he is a prisoner and can't help it. And yet they have beaten us fairly, beaten us all to pieces, beaten us so easily that we are objects of contempt even to their commonest private soldiers, with no shirts to hang out of the holes in their pantaloons, and cartridge-boxes tied round their waists with strands of rope. ♦

RAGGED REBELS

SUCH A LEADER
BY
VISCOUNT GARNET JOSEPH WOLSELEY
FIELD MARSHAL OF THE ENGLISH ARMY

In the fall of 1862--sometime between mid-September and mid-October--Sir Wolseley visited the American South. He was sympathetic to the Southern position in the Civil War and curious to see its armies in the field and to meet its commanders. Upon his return to England he wrote, anonymously under the byline "An English Officer," a description of his travels in Virginia for the January 1863 edition of BLACKWOOD'S EDINBURGH MAGAZINE. *Curiously, though his visit was in late September or early October of 1862, a month or so before Jackson's sitting for the famous full-beard "Winchester" portrait, Wolseley describes a Jackson appearing much like the man of the earlier Jackson portraits who wore side-burns, but no beard or mustache.*

Sir Wolseley, who was born June 4, 1833, eventually became the commander-in-chief of the English army. He died March 25, 1913.

. . . [W]e drove to Bunker's [sic] Hill . . . at which place Stonewall Jackson, now of world-wide celebrity, had his headquarters. With him we spent a most pleasant hour, and were agreeably surprised to find him very affable, having been led to expect that he was silent and almost morose. Dressed in his grey uniform, he looks like the hero that he is; and his thin compressed lips and calm glance, which meets yours unflinchingly, give evidence of that firmness and decision of character for which he is so famous. He has a broad open forehead, from which the hair is well brushed back; a shapely nose, straight, and rather long; thin colourless cheeks, with only a very small allowance of whisker; a cleanly-shaven upper lip and chin; and a pair of fine greyish-blue eyes, rather sunken, with overhanging brows, which intensify the keenness of his gaze, but without imparting any fierceness to it. Such are the general characteristics of his face; and I have only to add that a smile seems always lurking about his mouth

COURTESY *THE ILLUSTRATED LONDON NEWS*

STONEWALL JACKSON

This sketch (woodcut) from an English newspaper was clearly drawn after the 1851 Brady photograph, which was embellished with the same collar insignia (see page 24) shown here. The Brady photograph was popular as a *carte de visite* in England as well as in America.

when he speaks; and that though his voice partakes slightly of that harshness which Europeans unjustly attribute to *all* Americans, there is much unmistakable cordiality in his manner; and to us he talked most affectionately of England, and of his brief but enjoyable sojourn there. The religious element seems strongly developed in him; and though his conversation is perfectly free from all puritanical cant, it is evident that he is a person who never loses sight of the fact that there is an omnipresent Deity ever presiding over the minutest occurrences of life, as well as over the most important. Altogether, as one of his soldiers said to me in talking of him, "he is a glorious fellow!" and after I left him, I felt that I had at last solved the mystery of [the] Stonewall Bri[gade], and discovered why it was that it had accomplished such almost miraculous feats. With such a leader men would go anywhere, and face any amount of difficulties; and for myself, I believe that inspired by the presence of such a man, I should be perfectly insensible to fatigue, and reckon upon success as a moral certainty. ♦

COURTESY *THE ILLUSTRATED LONDON NEWS*

JACKSON IN WINTER DRESS

According to *The Illustrated London News* (February 13, 1863), this is "a sketch recently taken by our Special Artist in the Confederate camp." The "Special Artist" was presumably the paper's correspondent Frank Vizetelly, who wrote in a piece accompanying this drawing that ". . . General Jackson has acquired such a fame . . . that it is sad to think what would happen if the one life round which prestige clings should yield to a stray bullet or to the chance of disease."

HURRAH FOR JACKSON!
BY
"L.H.V."
THE LIBERTY HALL VOLUNTEERS
FOURTH VIRGINIA REGIMENT
STONEWALL BRIGADE

The following poem appeared in the October 2, 1862, issue of the LEXINGTON GAZETTE, *the hometown paper of many of the Liberty Hall Volunteers and their commander Stonewall Jackson.*

Awake to the song, give ear to the story,
How heroes have marched o'er the battle-field plain,
How commanders maintaining our national glory,
Have filled up the field with the enemies slain.

How Jackson the STONEWALL to enemies who would plunder
The wealth of our country, our freedom, our all,
Has given a lesson in the cannon's deep thunder
And thrown o'er their schemes despondency's pall.

All hail to the hero! he sought not his glory.
Give honor to him to whom honor is due.
He earned all his fame on the field, red and gory,
And fought for our freedom both brave and true.

He speaks to his comrades, "Come rush to the rescue,
Regardless of hardships, of danger and pain.
Your interest, your duty, your country now calls you,
Come meet the invader on mountain and plain!"

Then rush to the rescue, regardless of danger!
Strike, strike for your country before 'tis too late.
Before we'll be conquered, we'll fight till the stranger
Shall wander mid ruins of homes desolate.

Come on bold invader! Come on with your legions!
Onward to victory shall be the watchword.
Your conquest shall be over desolate regions,
Your welcome, *be it ever* to fire and sword.
--L.H.V.

COURTESY SHORNE HARRISON
STONEWALL
This engraving (from the Winchester photograph) was sold after the war to raise funds to build a monument to Jackson's memory at the Virginia Military Institute in Lexington, Virginia.

PART IV

CHANCELLORSVILLE

LEE AND JACKSON
BY
WALTER A. MONTGOMERY
PRIVATE, COMPANY A
TWELFTH NORTH CAROLINA REGIMENT

Walter Montgomery was born in Warrenton, North Carolina, in 1845, and so was only a boy when he entered the Confederate army in May 1861 at "scarcely ... a hundred pounds of weight, and only sixteen years and three months old." A year later, in May 1862, his unit was sent to "the Valley of Virginia" to reinforce General Jackson, "but on reaching Gordonsville, by rail, [they] learned of Jackson's success at McDowell, and retraced [their] movement to Hanover Court House." The next year, after a long march, Private Montgomery and his unit did eventually join the Army of Northern Virginia at the Wilderness. It was during this period that Montgomery saw both Lee and Jackson.

Walter Montgomery saw action from the Seven Days Battle to the surrender at Appomattox, eventually rising in the ranks to become a second lieutenant in Company F, Twelfth Carolina Regiment. He practiced law after the war and died in Raleigh in 1921.

. . . [This is] an incident which I witnessed at Spottsylvania. . . . Near the McCool house, at the base of the Horse Shoe Salient [May 12, 1864] the first line of Confederate troops was driven from the field in confusion. General Ewell, who was on the spot, personally engaged in trying to rally the men, lost his head, and with loud curses was using his sword on the backs of some of the flying soldiers. Just then General Lee rode up, and said: "General Ewell, you must restrain yourself; how can you expect to control these men when you have lost control of yourself? If you cannot repress your excitement, you had better retire." Then General Lee, in the quietest manner, moved among the men, and through their officers reformed the broken ranks.

One other incident of my army life, when I heard General Jackson's voice for the first and last time, will constitute my whole experience directly connected with those two great officers. When the battle of Chancellorsville was about to open [probably April 29, 1863], my regiment was in position near Hamilton's Crossing, watching Franklin's U.S. Corps cross [the] Rappahannock River, a little below Fredericksburg, a feint preparatory to Hooker's movement higher up the river.

General Jackson, with his staff, rode up to our command and asked the officer commanding for an officer and forty or fifty men for particular service near the Cedar Road. Sharpshooters of the brigade, under Lieutenant Moseley of my company, were assembled, and General Jackson told Moseley, in a few words, what he wanted done and where he wanted him to go. Moseley spoke up, when General Jackson seemed to intend to go with the party himself, saying, "General, you need not go; I know what you want, I will do it. I have been picketing in that section and know almost every rock and rail on the Cedar Road." The General replied, "Lieutenant, come go with me: when I post you, then I'll know you are there." Moseley told me afterwards the incident not only gave him a good lesson, but showed him the keynote of Jackson's military success--personal supervision over important tactical movements. ♦

&

MOST OF OUR OFFICERS HAVE A GREAT FEAR OF JACKSON. THAT HE IS THE MOST ABLE GENERAL ON THIS CONTINENT, NO ONE CAN DISPUTE.
--D.M. DRECKE, UNION SOLDIER,
FROM AN AUGUST 26, 1862, LETTER TO HIS FATHER

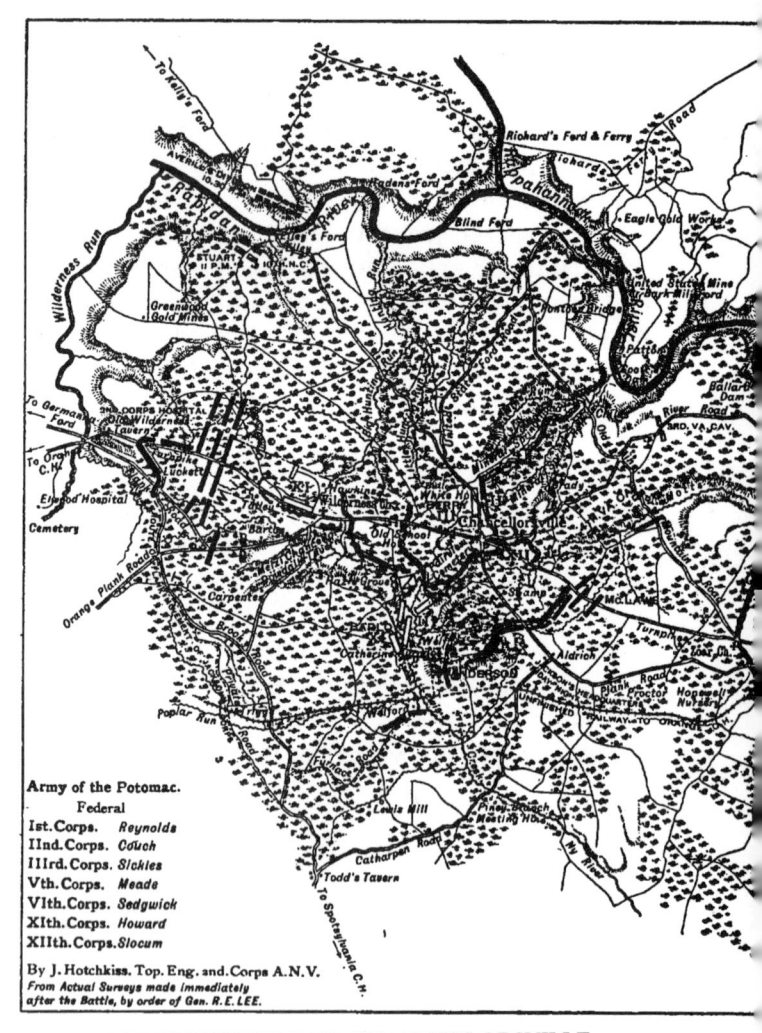

FREDERICKSBURG TO CHANCELLORSVILLE

On December 13, 1862, Jackson commanded the Confederate right wing during the battle of Fredericksburg. The following spring during the battle of Chancellersville, Jackson made a flanking movement (May 2, 1863) and surprised and routed O. O. Howard's corps from the field. On the evening of May 2, Jackson was wounded by his own men while reconnoitering his front lines. The wounding made necessary the amputation of his left arm. While recovering, pneumonia set in and he died of complications on the 10th of May in 1863.

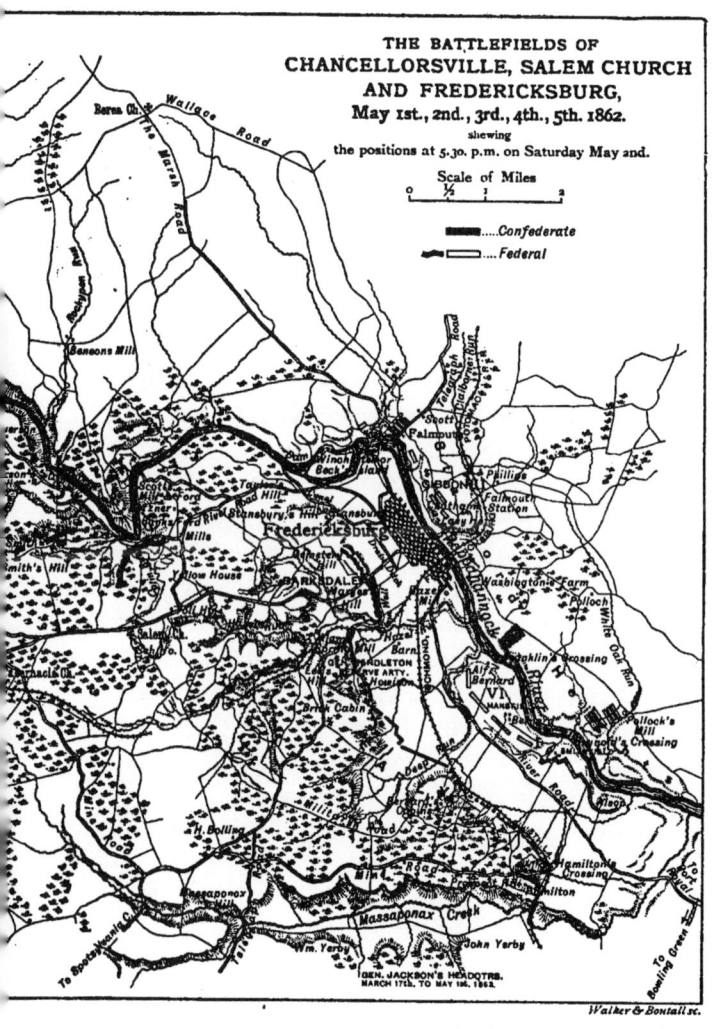

WE COULD NOT CHEER
BY
DAVID ELDRED HOLT

"... [T]he Southern soldiers," *wrote Walter Montgomery, "were indifferent in their feelings toward their government, [but] they respected and honored their military leaders, who praised their valor and shared their dangers. For General Jackson they had always cheers in battle and camp...." Well, not always, for as much as the men loved to cheer Jackson, they could not when the enemy was near. David Holt remembered into his old age how difficult it was to remain silent when Stonewall passed down the lines.*

As we halted on the side of the road in line of battle facing toward the river [May 1, 1863], word was passed up from our right along the line that, "Old Jax was coming and we must not cheer." Presently he came in sight on his little sorrel pony. He carried his cap in his hand. We waved our hats and some of the men shed tears. Of course I did. My heart was always in my throat. When he came to the Sixteenth Mississippi Regiment he stopped and looked along the line. Then he rode up to the flag and asked: "Is this the Sixteenth Mississippi?" Many voices answered: "Yes, sir." He said: "You were with me in the valley and around Richmond, and I remember well your gallant services. We are going to have some hard work here, and I have confidence in you and believe you will do your full part."

He rode on, and we could not cheer.... ♦

THREE GENERALS AT CHANCELLORSVILLE
BY
ANDREW DAVIDSON LONG

Andy Long lost both his brothers, Henry and Frank, in the Civil War. Henry was fatally wounded at Chancellorsville and Andy saw Jackson in the field hospital there when he went to visit his dying brother. "Jackson was shot Saturday night," he wrote, "and Henry was shot, through the groin, Sunday morning. It was mean weather, cold and frosty." In the piece below Andy describes an event which took place very shortly before the fighting at Chancellorsville began.

Just before I went into battle at Chancellorsville I stood in line of march, standing at rest, with my company, about 15 feet from Lee, Jackson, and Stuart. Lee came from the south, Jackson from the north and Stuart came from the east, from towards Fredericksburg.

These generals conferred together for a short time--perhaps ten minutes. They could not talk long for Joe Hooker was crossing the Rappahannock River on pontoons and Howard was crossing from close to Fredericksburg. I could draw a picture today of this conference. Jackson had his leg thrown around his saddle horn--a characteristic position for him to take. His cap was not pulled down very closely over his eyes as he frequently wore it. . . . His keen eyes were taking in the whole situation. (He had the keenest eyes I ever saw in a man.) . . . Jackson was not very closely trimmed. I was looking at him from his right side--his sorrel horse facing south. Lee was facing Jackson looking north. He was on his iron-grey horse, "Traveller," presented to him by a man in [West] Virginia. He had on his large grey hat. His partially grey beard was neatly trimmed. He was the best proportioned and finest looking man I ever saw. He was as straight as an arrow and a fine horseman. General Stuart rode up to Lee and Jackson--facing me. None of our men could hear the conversation. [The generals] looked over some maps hurriedly.

When they got through[,] Jackson went north to attack Hooker's right wing. . . . Lee went to Hooker's front and Stuart took the left wing. Here we whipped Joe Hooker. ♦

TWO MEN ON CRACKER BOXES
BY
JAMES POWER SMITH
CORPORAL IN THE ROCKBRIDGE ARTILLERY
STONEWALL BRIGADE
AND LATER
CAPTAIN AND ASSISTANT ADJUTANT-GENERAL
GENERAL T.J. JACKSON'S STAFF

By May 1, 1863, the Confederate divisions of Generals Anderson and McLaws, which Lee had sent from Fredericksburg toward Chancellorsville, had established defensive positions to resist the advance of Hooker from Chancellorsville. When, on the morning of May 1, Jackson arrived on the scene--ahead of his corps--he attacked with the divisions of Anderson and McLaws. The Federals then retreated to prepared positions around Chancellorsville.

General Lee, having already split his army once but willing to risk doing so again, conferred with Jackson on the evening of May 1 and decided that they must attack Hooker the next day at Chancellorsville. The only unresolved question was where. Hooker's left and center seemed very strong, but when J.E.B. Stuart brought word that Hooker's right was "in the air" the decision was made to split the army again and for Jackson, by a hidden march of about 12 miles, to hit Hooker (O.O. Howard's corps) on the flank.

The council between Lee and Jackson continued throughout the evening of May 1, and, as told in later years by Jackson's former aide James Power Smith in the following story, also during the early hours of May 2.

Smith was a divinity student at Hampden-Sydney College at the beginning of the Civil War and, later, a corporal of the Rockbridge Artillery when Jackson asked him to join his staff. After the war, James Smith became Reverend Smith, a Presbyterian minister.

. . . [A] mile and a half from Hooker's lines . . . at the fork of [two] roads General Lee and General Jackson spent the night, resting on the pine straw, curtained only by the close shadow of the pine forest. A little after nightfall I was sent by General Lee upon an errand to A.P. Hill, on the old stone turnpike a mile or two north; and returning some time later with information of matters on our right, I found General Jackson retired to rest, and

COUNCIL OF WAR

W. L. SHEPPARD

"... I saw, bending over a scant fire of twigs, two men seated on old cracker boxes and warming their hands over the little fire. I had to rub my eyes and collect my wits to recognize the figures of Robert E. Lee and Stonewall Jackson."

JAMES POWER SMITH

General Lee sleeping at the foot of a tree, covered with his army cloak. As I aroused the sleeper, he slowly sat up on the ground and said, "Ah, Captain, you have returned, have you? Come here and tell me what you have learned on the right." Laying his hand on me he drew me near him in a fatherly way that told of his warm and kindly heart. When I had related such information as I had secured for him, he thanked me for accomplishing his commission. . . . . . I went off to make a bed of my saddle-blanket, and, with my head in my saddle, near my horse's feet, was soon wrapped in the heavy slumber of a wearied soldier.

Some time after midnight I was awakened by the chill of the early morning hours, and, turning over, caught a glimpse of a little flame on the slope above me, and sitting up to see what it meant, I saw, bending over a scant fire of twigs, two men seated on old cracker boxes and warming their hands over the little fire. I had but to rub my eyes and collect my wits to recognize the figures of Robert E. Lee and Stonewall Jackson. Who can tell the story of that quiet council of war between two sleeping armies? Nothing remains on record to tell of plans discussed, and dangers weighed, and a great purpose formed, but the story of the great day so soon to follow. ♦

THE LAST TIME I SAW HIM
BY
ALLEN CHRISTIAN REDWOOD

"Lee and Jackson continued to examine the possibilities [for attack on the enemy], exchanging ideas, pondering their practicalities, revising, estimating, speculating about Federal lines and strengths and purposes. Then Stuart rode up through the moonlight to them. He had something to report."

The last time my eyes were to behold him--how well it comes to mind!--was upon the morning of the fateful May 2, 1863, before the close of which day was to be ended his career as a soldier. We were moving out by the flank on a little woodland road, where we had been in bivouac the night before; it was a gloomy, overcast morning, as if giving premonition of the calamity to come to us before the next rising of the sun. Before we reached the plank road, in a small opening among the pines were two mounted figures whom we recognized as Lee and Jackson. The former was seemingly giving some final instructions, emphasizing with the forefinger of his gantleted right hand in the palm of the left what he was saying--inaudible to us. The other, wearing a long rubber coat over his uniform (it had been raining a little, late in the night), was nodding vivaciously all the while. ♦

E. B. D. JULIO, 1869

THE LAST MEETING

"... [I]n a small opening among the pines were two mounted figures whom we recognized as Lee and Jackson."

– *ALLEN CHRISTIAN REDWOOD*

"PRESS ON; PRESS ON"
BY
HUNTER HOLMES MCGUIRE

  Never can I forget the eagerness and intensity of Jackson on that march to Hooker's rear [Chancellorsville, May 2, 1863]. His face was pale, his eyes flashing. Out from his thin, compressed lips came the terse command: "Press forward, press forward." In his eagerness, as he rode, he leaned over on the neck of his horse as if in that way the march might be hurried. "See that the column is kept closed and that there is no straggling," he more than once ordered, and "Press on, press on," was repeated again and again. Every man in the ranks knew that we were engaged in some great flank movement, and they eagerly responded and pressed on at a rapid gait. Fitz Lee met us and told Jackson he could show him the whole of Hooker's army if he went with him to the top of a hill near by. They went together and Jackson carefully inspected through his glasses the Federal command. . . . [O]n his return . . . he ordered one aide to go forward and tell General Rodes, who was in the lead, to cross the Plank Road and go straight on to the Turnpike, and another aide to go to the rear of the column and see that it was kept closed up, and all along the line he repeatedly said: "Press on; press on."

  The fiercest energy possessed the man, and the fire of battle fell strong upon him. . . . ♦

WHERE STONEWALL WAS WOUNDED
BY
ALEXANDER TEDFORD BARCLAY
LIBERTY HALL VOLUNTEERS
FOURTH VIRGINIA REGIMENT
STONEWALL BRIGADE

Alexander Tedford Barclay, III ("Ted") was born May 16, 1844, at "Sycamore" near Lexington, Virginia. In the spring of 1861, when he was 17, he enlisted in the Confederate army as part of the Liberty Hall Volunteers.

Ted Barclay fought as part of the Stonewall Brigade as a private until November 1863, when he was promoted from private to first lieutenant for "gallantry on [the] field" at Mine Run. He was taken prisoner at Spotsylvania in May 1864 (when the Stonewall Brigade was destroyed) and finally released in July 1865. After the war he was a newspaper editor in Rockbridge County, Virginia.

On Friday, May 8, 1863, Ted Barclay wrote the letter below to his folks in Lexington; in it he tells of the Battle of Chancellorsville, which had taken place the week before.

Dear Ones at Home,

I suppose that you think that it is time I was writing if in the land of the living, but after I give you an account of my wanderings for the last ten or twelve days I think you will acquit me of any intentional delay. We left our old camp on Tuesday the 28th of April, marched to Hamilton's Crossing and stayed all night, and the next day and night under the shelling of the enemy's cannon stationed on Stafford Heights. Soon, on the morning of the 30th, we left Hamilton's in a dense fog, which concealed our movements, moved up the river, Rappahannock, ten or twelve miles, driving the enemy slowly before us. Camped that night in an open field, all feeling that on the morrow we would have to engage the enemies of our country and mankind. On the morning of May 1st, we moved slowly up the road, shelling occasionally to find out the position of the enemy. About twelve o'clock we had driven in all their pickets and found the main body of the enemy stationed behind formidable breastworks, their front defended by abatis of felled trees, which, I suppose, our Generals thought too strong to attack, so Gen. Jackson taking a column [on May 2] commenced a flank movement to their [*the Union*] right through a dense pine forest, Gen. Stuart clearing the road as we advanced. After three or four hours we found our division a mile in the rear of the enem[y]'s line which extended across the Orange and Fredericksburg plank road forming in line of battle. Gen. A.P. Hill on the left, our division commanded by General [R.E.] Colston on the right. We advanced down the plank road, our line being three or four miles in length. Presently the sharp rattle of the musket told plainly that the pickets had commenced the engagement, which was to be the greatest defeat the Federal army ever had and which was to cost us so many valuable lives. We came out of the woods, which had been concealing our movements, into an open field expecting every moment to engage the enemy, but they were so much taken by surprise that our pickets had driven their whole line, capturing one battery and about 500 prisoners. . . . We continued driving their rear until nine o'clock at night, having crossed one line of breastworks which the enemy had hastily thrown up. After we got in their rear, lying down behind their breastworks, we intended waiting until morning to renew the fight; but the enemy thinking to retrieve himself made a night attack [in] which

A. C. REDWOOD

WOUNDED

"All my wounds are from my own men. . . ."
— *STONEWALL JACKSON,* AS HE LAY WOUNDED AT CHANCELLORSVILLE, LATE EVENING OF MAY 2, 1863

they partially succeeded in capturing one of our batteries, but soon we were in line again and recaptured our battery together with quite a number of prisoners. Twas in this fight that Gen. Jackson lost his arm. . . .

The next morning every one knew that the most terrible battle of the war must begin. We marched slowly down the road, all the time under fire of several batteries of the enemy. We at first went on the left of the plank road, thinking that the main body of the enemy were posted there, but soon we found out from the pressure on our right that it was the enemy's strongest point, so we had to cross the road covered by the enemy's cannon, [and] here many a noble Southron fell to rise no more, among them Gen. Paxton who was shot through the heart from which he died shortly afterwards. A piece of shell struck my knapsack, but was too spent to hurt me. We went about a quarter of a mile to the left and took position behind the front line of the enemy's breastworks from which they had just before been driven. As soon as we were in line, our guns primed and bayonets fixed, Gen. Stuart, he being in command of the Corps, Gens. Jackson and Hill both wounded, called out for the Old Stonewall [Brigade] to follow. We went over the breastworks with a yell which was answered by a shower of leaden hail. Feeling that perhaps at that time prayers were going up at home for our protection I became almost unconscious of danger though men were falling fast and thick around me. We halted and commenced firing at the enemy about one hundred yards distant, we stood and fired until almost every man was killed or wounded; the force of the enemy being so much greater than ours. Major Terry, commanding our regiment, gave the order to fall back, but I was totally unconscious of what was going on and tried to rally the men, when Major Terry came up to me and ordered me to fall back as nearly all his regiment were killed or wounded.

This letter is already too long but I could write more if I had time. . . .

TED

WOUNDING OF JACKSON

Perhaps the unknown engraver has failed to "reverse" the original painting; for it appears here that Jackson has been wounded in the right, not the left, arm.

"THE BRIGADE MUST NOT KNOW"
BY
ANONYMOUS

"... *Stonewall Jackson was killed by his own men. He rode through the picket lines at Chancellorsville, and gave orders that they must fire on any who came along their road, not expecting to return that way himself; but changing his mind afterward, his men, obedient to orders, poured a volley of shot into the little group of officers and men.... As they bore General Jackson to the rear ... he said to the officer who had him in charge, 'The brigade must not know, sir, that I am wounded.'" The following is an anonymous poem.*

"Who've ye got there?" --"Only a dying brother,
Hurt in the front just now."
"Good boy! he'll do. Somebody tell his mother
Where he was killed, and how."

"Whom have you there?" --"A crippled courier, major,
Shot by mistake, we hear.
He was with Stonewall." --"Cruel work they've made here:
Quick with him to the rear!"

"Well, who comes next?" --"Doctor, speak low, sir;
Don't let the men find out."
"It's *Stonewall*! God!" --"The brigade must not know, sir,
While there's a foe about."

Whom have we *here*--shrouded in martial manner,
Crowned with a martyr's charm?
A grand dead hero in a living banner,
Born of his heart and arm.

The heart whereon his cause hung--see how clingeth
That banner to his bier!
The arm wherewith his cause struck--hark! how ringeth
His trumpet in their rear!

What have we left? His glorious inspiration,
His prayers in council met.
Living, he laid the first stones of a nation;
And dead, he builds it yet. ⌘

JACKSON'S STAFF

The staff, starting at "one o'clock" and going clockwise, are Maj. Dabney, Lt. Col. Allan, Lt. Col Pendleton, Capt. Morrison, Maj. Bridgeford, Maj. Douglas, Capt. Smith, Maj. McGuire, Capt. Hotchkiss, Maj. Hawks.

WE HAD LOST JACKSON
BY
BERRY GREENWOOD BENSON

Here Sergeant Benson describes the first days of May 1863, at Chancellorsville.

... [W]e listened to the roar of the battle, which gradually grew fainter, as did the yells of the Confederates, so we knew that our men were still driving the enemy and that the victory was ours. But we had lost Jackson, struck down by our own men, in that volley which had made us jump so quick the night before.

Never more would we follow him to battle, never again would he be cursed by his own men for his hard marching, never again so wildly cheered by the same men as he galloped by them. For I have heard men, worn out by a break-neck march, cursing Jackson bitterly, yet all the while they worshipped him, and could not have been bribed to drop out of the ranks. . . . .

And now Jackson lay mortally wounded, his brilliant story drawing to a close. . . . Such gloom therefor [*sic*] as fell upon the people! ♦

&

". . . [W]HEN A TEACHER ENTERS THE CLASSROOM, WEARING A 'COPPERHEAD' AS A BADGE, AND WHEN THAT TEACHER SHROUDS THAT BREASTPIN IN BLACK ON LEARNING OF THE DEATH OF THE TRAITOR JACKSON, THE QUESTION ARISES WHETHER SUCH A COURSE OF CONDUCT OUGHT TO BE TOLERATED. OUR FRIENDS ARE SACRIFICING THEIR LIVES TO SAVE THEIR COUNTRY, AND HERE IS A *SHE-CESH* TEACHER IN FULL SYMPATHY WITH THE REBELLION. . . ."

--TENTH ANNUAL REPORT OF THE SUPERINTENDENT OF COMMON SCHOOLS OF THE STATE OF MAINE

THIS IS CALLED THE BATTLE OF CHANCELLORSVILLE
BY
GEORGE W. KOONTZ
PRIVATE, RICE'S BATTERY
MCINTOSH'S BATTALION

George W. Koontz wrote to his cousin Mattie a week after the Battle of Chancellorsville.

Camp near Hamilton's Crossing
6 Miles South Fredericksburg Va
Sunday night May 10/63

Dear Mattie:

Your kind and interesting letter was received Tuesday week last, and I would have answered sooner but on Wednesday 29 April we received orders to march. And by 12 o'clock we were on the march for Hamilton's Crossing (20 miles distant from our old camp at Bowling Green). We traveled on sticking in the mud and pulling out again. We proceeded until 2 or 3 o'clock in the night. When it commenced raining we had to stop. Day light found us sticking in the mud with the road blockaded with Wagons & Artillery al[l the] way to Hamilton's [Crossing] which was two miles. Well we got started again and about 10 we were brought up on the hills, near the old battlefield of the 13th Dec. and were ordered into Camp. The enemy had crossed the river, and we were expecting to go to fighting. Shots were exchanged very freely and we expected to be into it next morning (Friday). But Friday morning came--instead of fighting everything was comparatively quiet. We were order[ed] to take up line of march. We did not

MEN OF STONEWALL'S CORPS AT HAMILTON'S CROSSING

A. C. REDWOOD

know where but we did not travel far before we could hear the roar of Cannon in the distan[ce] and it was reported that the enemy had crossed at Kelly's ford, which was true. We moved on up towards Orange on the plank road and where we camped. Our advance had driven the Yankee advance back so I may say that I slept on the edge of a battlefield.

Everything was quiet during the night, but when Saturday morning came it brought with it a thundering of Artillery and we were ordered to the front. About 10 the cannonading ceased and I found that our men had driven the enemy again. I soon discovered that Genl. Jackson was turning the enem[y's] right flank, and about 5 or six we had completely gotten in their rear, drove them from their entrenchments, [and] run them I suppose 3 or 4 miles. Night coming on brought the fight for the day to a close but the[re] was firing of Infantry and heavy firing of Artillery nearly the whole night. That was another night spent upon the battlefield among dead and wounded. We had as yet lost but very few men and I could not have much sympathy for the Yankees.

Soon after dark on Saturday evening was when Genl. Jackson, [Genl.] Hill and Col. Crutchfield, our chief of artillery, w[ere] wounded. Genl. Jackson had to have his left arm amputated. They were wounds by our own men. He was riding between our first and second lines of battle and was mistaken for Yankee Cavalry.

Sunday morning came and the hardest day's fight. The Yankees had secured a good position. As soon as day came heavy and desperate firing commenced. We were ordered up pretty soon and soon we were ordered to take position within 3/4 mile of the enem[y's] Batteries under a very heavy rain of Shot and Shell. We fired about an hour and a half, exhausting nearly all our a[m]munition, but we did not cease firing until we drove the enemy from and took possession of their position. We had one man, Corporal James D. Long, killed and eight wounded, the greater portion slight wounds. All the boys that you are acquainted with came out al[l] right.

We remained in and about [*in the area of*] the last day's (Sunday) fighting ground until Wednesday, when we returned here, but during this time the enemy had forced our men--what was left (1 Division) at Fredericksburg--to retire and Genl. Lee had to return and drive them back across the river, which he did on Monday evening and Tuesday morning. So old Fighting Joe [Hooker] made good his escape perhaps never to return. The loss[es] on both sides were very heavy but I firmly believe the Yankees['] loss was two to our one if not more. Some say five to one. I never saw the like of Knapsacks, &c. The ground was literal[l]y covered from where we started them [*that is, from where the Confederates began to force the Yankees to retreat*] until we stop[p]ed.

The Fredericksburg fight of Dec. 13 was not a circumstance compared to this--that was nothing more than play. We had miserable bad weather connected with it which made it so [much] more disagreeable. This is called the battle of "Chancellorsville."

I have given you as correct [an] account as I could sum up. I guess you will be able to gather more from the papers. I forgot to tell you

A. C. REDWOOD

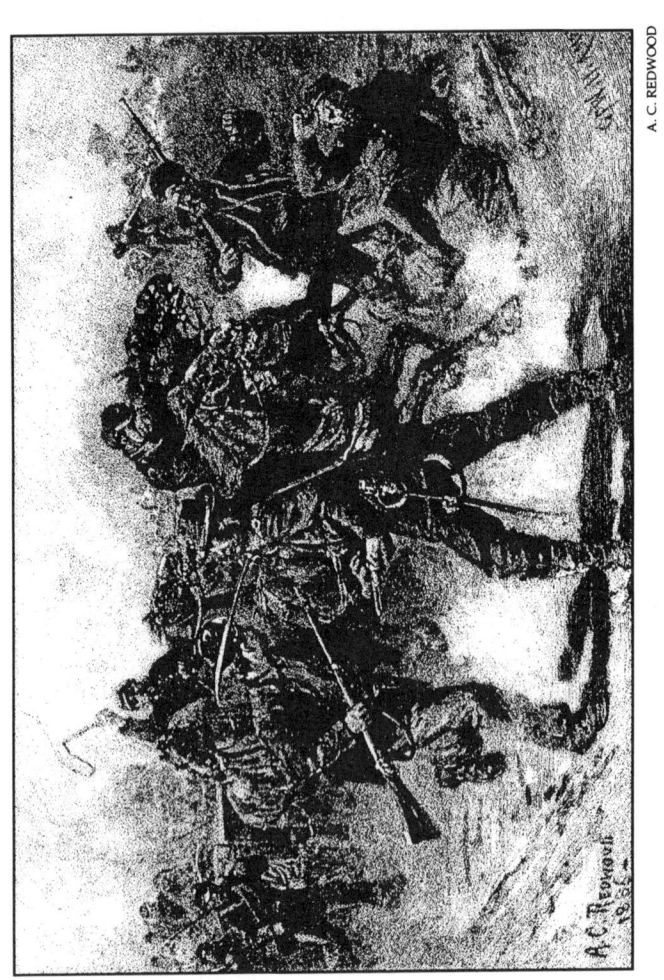

CHANCELLORSVILLE

Rodes' Division, Jackson's Corps, leads the charge during Jackson's flank attack at Chancellorsville (May 2, 1863) and rolls up O. O. Howard's Corps.

that the [area] of Country fought over from begin[n]ing to end I think will exceed 20 miles. I will stop writing of the fight.

I guess we will not get back to our old Camp at Bowling Green, though I would like to go back there.

The boys are well. . . . I send a piece of Gray Cloth by Mr. Coffman. . . . I want to have a coat made. . . . <u>My love to all</u>.

It is twelve and I must close--"All Quiet along the Rappahanock Tonight"--[*The next sentence is squeezed in between this last line and Koontz's signature.*] It was reported this evening in Camp that Genl. Jackson died from his wounds, but I don't believe [it] & I hope it is not true.

Write soon to your Cousin,
GEO. W. KOONTZ

&

A DEEP GLOOM IS OVER THE CAMP BECAUSE OF THE DEATH OF GEN. JACKSON. HE WAS TAKEN AWAY FROM US BECAUSE WE MADE ALMOST AN IDOL OF HIM. . . .
--TED BARCLAY, MAY 12, 1863

STONEWALL JACKSON
An engraving from a painting by L. M. D. Guillaume

THE DEATH OF JACKSON
BY
JOHN OVERTON CASLER
PRIVATE, COMPANY A
33RD VIRGINIA REGIMENT
STONEWALL BRIGADE

John O. Casler was born in Gainsboro, Frederick County, Virginia (near Winchester), on December 1, 1838, but was raised in Springfield, (now West) Virginia. In March 1859, when he was 21, he "took Horace Greeley's advice to 'Go West and grow up with the country.'" He went to Missouri where he stayed until the spring of 1861, when he heard the rumors of war and decided he should return home. On his way back to Virginia, Casler learned of the firing on Fort Sumter and knew "that war had commenced."

At home again, he joined a company called the "Potomac Guards," which eventually became part of the Stonewall Brigade. Casler served as a private throughout the war, participating in battle after battle, from First Manassas to the surrender. He was wounded, taken prisoner, and in the last year of the war transferred to the 11th Virginia Cavalry.

After the war Casler moved to Oklahoma where he remained active in Confederate veterans' affairs.

General Jackson was taken to a private house near Guinea Station, the best physicians attending him, and his wife and daughter (Miss Julia, then [just] months old) came to see him. Our old brigade would inquire after him every day, and the news was that he was doing well, and we thought that he would soon be with us. But alas! vain hope! death is no respecter of persons, and we were doomed never to see him again. He suddenly got worse, and died on the 10th of May, 1863. We were terribly shocked, for we thought from what we had heard that he would surely recover.

A great many of our boys said then that our star of destiny would fade, and that our cause would be lost without Jackson, as there was no General who could execute a flank movement with so much secrecy and surprise as he could. So it proved to be; but the war might have ended the same as it did had he lived. Though the destiny of a nation may appear to be in one man's hands sometimes, yet there is One above all who controls both men and nations.

But I believed at the time, and believe now, and always shall believe, that if we had had Jackson with us at the battle of Gettysburg he would have flanked the enemy off those heights with his corps, if he had to take one day's rations and go around Washington City to get there. He would have found his rear if he had any. . . .

General Stuart had reported to [General Jackson] that a considerable force had crossed the river above Chancellorsville, and threatened his left. He then sent one brigade up there after dark with orders to form a line when they came in view of the Federals, to fire three volleys and then return and take their places in line of battle. They did so, and the consequence was the force of Federals at that ford remained there during the next two days' fight, fortifying their position for fear of an attack. Such was the strategy of "Stonewall." Shortly after he was wounded, and when the enemy were rushing up fresh troops, General Pender told him that his men were in such confusion that he feared he would not be able to hold his ground.

"General Pender," said Jackson, "you *must* keep your men together and hold your ground."

This was the last military order ever given by Jackson. The last sentence he ever uttered was, "Let us pass over the river and rest under the shade of the trees."

Before his death he sent General Lee word that he had lost his left arm. General Lee replied that he (Lee) had lost his right arm in losing him.

He inquired minutely about the battle and the different troops engaged, and his face would light up with enthusiasm when told how his old brigade acted, and he uttered "Good, good" with unwonted energy when the gallant behavior of the "Stonewall Brigade" was alluded to. He said: "The men of the brigade will be, some day, proud to say to their children, 'I was one of the Stonewall Brigade.' They are a noble body of men."

Just before he died he seemed to be caring for his soldiers, and giving such directions as these: "Tell Major Hawks to send forward provisions to the men; order A.P. Hill to prepare for action. Pass the infantry to the front."

MAJOR HAWKS

After his death[,] orders came to the "Stonewall Brigade" to be in readiness to march to the house where Jackson lay a corpse and escort the remains to the railroad depot, to be sent to Richmond. The brigade rigged up in the best they had, cleaned their arms and were anxious to go, and [were] kept waiting impatiently until, finally, the order was countermanded and we did not get to see him.

We all thought very hard of it, for we wished to show our respect for our beloved commander, and gaze on his face once more; but that small privilege was denied us. His only escort were some doctors and officials who never had followed him in battle, while the men who had followed him from Harper's Ferry to Chancellorsville had to lie idle in camp.

The news of the wounding of General Jackson filled the army with the most profound and undisguised grief. His men loved him devotedly, and he was the idol of the whole army.

Many stout-hearted veterans, who had, under his guidance, borne hardships and privations innumerable, and dangers the most appalling, without a murmur, wept like children when told that their idolized General was no more. The death of General Jackson was communicated to the army by General Lee in the following order:

>Headquarters
>Army Northern Virginia, May 11, 1863.
>General Order No. 61.
>
>With deep grief the commanding General announces to the army the death of Lieutenant General T.J. Jackson, who expired on the 10th instant, at quarter past 3 p.m. The daring, skill and energy of this great and good soldier, by the decree of an Allwise Providence, are now lost to us.
>
>But while we mourn his death we feel that his spirit still lives, and will inspire the whole army with his indomitable courage and unshaken confidence in God as our hope and strength.
>
>Let his name be a watchword to his corps, who have followed him to victory on so many fields.
>
>Let his officers and soldiers emulate his invincible determination to do everything in the defense of our beloved country.
>
>R. E. LEE, General

On Monday morning, the 11th of May, it was announced that the remains of General Jackson would reach Richmond during the day, and the Mayor of that city at once requested all persons to suspend business after 10 o'clock, in token of their respect for the departed hero. All stores, workshops, the government departments, and all places in which labor was performed, were closed. Flags were hung at half-mast and a deep silence reigned over the

GUINEA STATION

In this small office building in the yard of the Chandler home at Guinea Station, Stonewall Jackson spent his last days. He died here Sunday afternoon, May 10, 1863.

Capital of Virginia. Large crowds filled the streets, and, in spite of the intense heat, waited patiently for the arrival of the cars from Fredericksburg.

Shortly after 4 o'clock in the afternoon, the special train containing the precious burden moved slowly into the city. Only the solemn peal of the bells as they tolled their mournful knell broke the deep silence that reigned over everything.

At the depot the coffin was removed from the cars, and placed in a hearse to be carried to the mansion of the Governor. The escort which received it consisted of Major General Elzey and staff, the state guard of Virginia, with colors shrouded in mourning, the 44th North Carolina and the 1st Virginia Regiments (after which came the hearse and General Jackson's staff), the city authorities and citizens on foot.

The remains were escorted to the mansion of the Governor and placed in the reception parlor. The lid of the coffin was removed, the new flag of the Confederacy, which had never before been used for any purpose, was thrown over it, and a single wreath of laurel laid upon the lifeless breast.

During the evening his friends were allowed to visit the body. The only change that was perceptible was that the features seemed somewhat smaller than they were in life. But there was still the firm, grave expression which had always dwelt there, and, above all, there rested upon the lifeless countenance an expression of happiness and peace so perfect and so intense that the gazer was awed and thrilled by it.

During the night the body was embalmed and a plaster cast of his features taken in order that they might be preserved in marble.

The next day all the honors that his native state

could lavish upon her noble son were heaped upon him. At 11 o'clock his body was removed from the Executive Mansion and conveyed . . . to the Capitol of Virginia. . . .

. . . The streets were filled with large crowds. The mournful cortege moved on in silence, which was only broken by the solemn strains of music and the discharge of artillery at intervals of half an hour. Tears rolled down many cheeks, and hundreds who had known General Jackson only by his great deeds wept as though mourning for a brother. Such an outburst of grief had never been witnessed in Virginia since the death of Washington.

Upon the arrival of the procession at the square the column was halted, the body removed and borne into the capitol, where it la[y] in state, in the Hall of the House of Representatives of the Confederate States. At least twenty thousand persons visited the hall to behold the remains of the hero that day.

The next morning the remains were placed on a special train and conveyed to Lynchburg.

It was hoped that General Jackson would be buried in Hollywood Cemetery, near Richmond. There Virginia has prepared a last resting place for her honored children. There rest the ashes of Monroe and Tyler, and many of the good and brave of this revolution, and it was hoped that there, too, would rest the dust of General Jackson; but it was his wish to sleep in his dearly loved home in the Valley, and thither all that remained of him was carried. On Wednesday morning the remains passed through Lynchburg. Minute guns were fired, bells were tolled, and a large procession of citizens followed the body through the city. On Thursday afternoon they reached Lexington. They were met at the canal by the corps of cadets, the professors of the Institute, and a large number of citizens, and escorted to the Institute barracks. The body of General

Jackson was placed in the old lecture room which once had been his. Two years before he had left it an humble and almost unknown man; now he returned to it with the hero's laurel wreath encircling his brow and enshrined forever in the hearts of his countrymen.

With the exception of the heavy mourning drapery with which it was hung, the room was just as he had left it. It had not been occupied during his absence. The body was deposited just in front of the chair in which he used to sit. . . .

The next day, the 15th of May, General Jackson was buried in the cemetery at Lexington, Virginia. . . . ♦

THE STAINLESS BANNER
The second flag of the Confederacy was used for the first time to cover Stonewall Jackson's coffin.

IN HIS OLD SECTION ROOM
BY
SAMUEL BALDWIN HANNAH
CADET, VIRGINIA MILITARY INSTITUTE
CLASS OF 1863
AND LATER PRIVATE
14TH VIRGINIA CAVALRY

Samuel B. Hannah was born in Charlotte County, Virginia, on October 19, 1843. He entered Hampden-Sydney College at the age of 16, but left to join the Confederate army when the Civil War began. However, apparently persuaded to continue his education, he left the army and entered VMI on January 1, 1862, and graduated the next year. On August 6, 1863, he wrote the superintendent at VMI, General Smith, the following letter:

> "You will oblige me very much indeed by sending me a written Certificate of my graduation as I intend to leave for the Army & join the 14th Va. Cavalry as a private.... It would give me great pleasure to call upon you on my way to Lee's Army, but time will not allow it."

After the war, Samuel Hannah taught school, farmed, held a judge's seat on the county court, and became the first superintendent of public schools in West Virginia. Hannah died January 19, 1921, in West Virginia.

In the following excerpts from a letter written to his mother, the young cadet describes the happenings at VMI and in Lexington which took place when the body of Stonewall Jackson was brought home.

VMI Institute
May 17, [1863]

I was Officer of the Day when the body of Gen. Jackson was brought in Barracks; no military escort accompanied him from Richmond, only a few citizens, among them the Gov. His body was said to be embalmed, but of no avail. Decomposition had already taken place, in consequence of which his face was not exposed to view as the features were said not to be natural. The coffin was a perfect flower bed and under, that which was presented to his wife by the President, the first new Confederate flag ever made. His body was placed in his old Section room which will remain draped for six months.

Gen. Smith then requested that none of the flowers should be removed from the coffin, which was an impossibility although I had Sentinel posted over the remains. Still the Sentinels would remove things for themselves and of course they were afraid to inform on others for fear of being caught at it themselves. I did not think it right to take what others had placed there as a memorial of their love and esteem for our beloved Jackson, although I would prize a trophy like that the highest imaginable. Still, as it had been entrusted to me to see that all was kept right, so long as his body was under my charge I couldn't conscientiously take any of the flowers when I knew that every cadet was afraid to let me see him take [a flower] or touch the body.

He only remained in Barracks one day and night. He was buried on Friday the 15th of May. Dr. White preached his funeral; the old Gentleman seemed, and I know he was, deeply afflicted, for from all accounts, the Gen. took quite an active part in the church and was the founder of the Colored Sunday School and the main stay of it as long as he was in Lexington.

... I lament and hang my head in shame at the idea of not having the privilege and honor of calling myself one of the veterans of Jackson's Corps. . . . ♦

VMI CADETS AT STONEWALL JACKSON'S GRAVE
Ca. 1870, Lexington, Virginia

HONOR TO THE OLD HERO
BY
CHARLES THOMAS HAIGH
CADET, VIRGINIA MILITARY INSTITUTE
LATER PRIVATE AND THEN LIEUTENANT
COMPANY B, 37TH NORTH CAROLINA CAVALRY

Charles T. Haigh was born in Fayetteville, North Carolina, on March 23, 1845. He became a cadet at the age of 15, at the Hillsboro Military Academy, and when war began he was appointed a drillmaster at a camp in North Carolina. In the winter of 1861-1862 his father sent him to VMI to complete his education; he was at VMI when the Corps of Cadets was called out to reinforce Stonewall Jackson at McDowell in the spring of 1862. In July of 1863, after Stonewall's death and the Southern defeats at Gettysburg and Vicksburg, Haigh's father finally gave in to his son's pleas to be allowed to resign from VMI and go to the front where the boy knew he was needed. Charles volunteered as a private but was soon elected a lieutenant in Company B of the 37th North Carolina Cavalry. He fought at the Wilderness "with the coolness of a veteran," and also at the Battle of Spotsylvania Court House, where--in charging an enemy battery in the Bloody Angle--Charles Haigh was killed, reportedly shouting, "Charge, boys! Charge!" His comrades called him "brave and fearless," and his commander said of him that he was "gallant on the battlefield." The following are excerpts from Cadet Haigh's diary.

MONDAY MAY 11TH [1863]

The death of the lamented hero "Stonewall" Jackson is a terrible blow to the South. The news of his death reached us last night at midnight--his military career fills the brighest and most momentous pages of the history of our country and the achievements of our army. He departed life at Guinea Station last Sunday at 3¼ o'clock. His remains will be carried to Richmond where they will be in state for one day then brought here (Lexington) for interment.

WEDNESDAY MAY 13TH

All academic duties are suspended today in honor to the old hero. His body is expected hourly.

THURSDAY MAY 14TH
Gen. Jackson's body arrived by the boat at 1 o'clock--was escorted to Barracks by the Corps and placed in his Section room which room is draped in mourning for the period of six months. He is in a fine metallic coffin. The *first flag* made in the South of the new design covers his coffin--on the flag, wreaths of evergreens and flowers. It is the request of his wife that he shall be buried tomor[r]ow. Half hour guns have been firing from . . . his old battery.

FRIDAY MAY 15
Guns have been firing all morning in honor of the lamented Jackson.
FRIDAY AFTERNOON. The procession formed in front of the sally port at half past ten. Commenced to move at 11. Corps in front of caisson on which he was borne. Then a company of Cavalry, after that a company composed of all the wounded and all that were once members of the old Stonewall Brigade. Bells were tolling all over town. . . . ♦

COURTESY VIRGINIA MILITARY INSTITUTE ARCHIVES
CHARLES THOMAS HAIGH

⌘

COURTESY SHORNE HARRISON

T. J. JACKSON
by
Nast

PART V

EPILOGUE

SHORT *ONE* MAN
BY
ALLEN CHRISTIAN REDWOOD

After the Confederate success at Chancellorsville came Gettysburg. The question is often asked what would have happened had Jackson been present on that memorable field--Jackson, the man who was always up to time, if he brought but a fragment of his force with him, and whose "first musket on the ground was fired." As General Fitz Lee significantly related the case, "Suppose Jackson to have been four miles off the field [*at Gettysburg*] at midnight of July 1st [1863] and been advised that General Lee wished the key-point of the enemy's position attacked the next day; would the time of that attack have approximated more nearly to 4 A.M. or 4 P.M.?" --for answer, see the verse already quoted. For if the other corps commandrs did not "like to go into battle with one boot off," ours would, at a pinch, go in barefoot--but he got there!

In the discussions of the Gettysburg campaign which have come into notice since the event, much space has been given to the comparison of the relative forces of the two armies contending on that field. The disparity under the most liberal estimates inclines always in favor of the Federals, yet it seems to the writer that not enough account has been taken of the most significant shortage on the Confederate side of the balance. Successful battles had been waged and won more than once against greater odds, in point of mere numbers--as at Sharpsburg (Antietam) and Chancellorsville, for instance. But at Gettysburg, we were short just *one* man--who had been dead just two months-- and his name was "Stonewall" Jackson. ♦

LOSS AND SURRENDER
BY
WALTER MONTGOMERY

At Appomattox in April 1865, almost two years after his death, Stonewall Jackson was on the minds of the Confederate soldiers.

[The men] realized, not fully, it is true, but measurably, the tremendous importance of the event, and [began] to take thought for the future. Of course their first thought was to reach their homes as soon as possible, for their services were, in most cases, sorely needed there. Crops could be planted and cultivated by those whose lives had been formerly on the farms, and the others, in some indefinite way, hoped for something to do. Then, they wished to get through with the trying ordeal of the act of surrender, for they did not know what the formalities might be, and in spite of their great deeds of the past, and consciences at rest on the score of duty performed to the last, they yet felt that it would be to them a humiliating scene. There was no personal bitterness in their hearts, little or no profane language, no curses upon their enemies. Their conduct was equal to the occasion.

I heard no word of ill-will against the National Government in the future, no suggestion of guerilla warfare. The universal sentiment was that the question in dispute had been fought to a finish, and that was the end of it. Their confidence in their general officers was unshaken, and for General Lee their affection and their esteem amounted to adoration. They knew he was heartbroken. In discussing the incidents which produced the most harmful effects upon the fortunes of the army, they mentioned the death of General Jackson, and the failure to occupy the heights at Gettysburg at the conclusion of the first day's battle. ◆

THE OILCLOTH COAT
BY
JOSEPH BRYAN
PRIVATE, MOSBY'S PARTISAN RANGERS

Joseph Bryan was 19 years old when he enlisted in John S. Mosby's Partisan Rangers. Wounded soon after, he was furloughed home. During this furlough he came to possess the oilcloth coat Stonewall Jackson was wearing when he was mortally wounded. Below, Bryan tells how he found and purchased this historic garment, which is now on permanent display at the VMI Museum in Lexington, Virginia.

I was sent to my home in Fluvanna County in November 1864 (upon a wounded furlough) and took the opportunity to visit my sister, who was then refugeeing in Goochland County.

Just across the river, in Powhatan County, near "Balmead," my father had rented a farm in conjunction with Major J. Horace Lacy, who owned a large part of the battlefield of Chancellorsville.

To this place, as one of the greater security, they had both sent a number of their servants from their places in Spotsylvania and Gloucester Counties, which had been overrun by the enemy. I went to this place to see my old colored friends, and there met a Mr. Jones, the overseer, who had come with Major Lacy's servants from the Wilderness, and who was in charge of this place.

It was a rainy day, and some complaint being made of the disagreeable weather, Jones remarked that he had an oil-cloth overcoat which had kept him dry in pouring rain, all day.

I instantly protested against such a treasure being left in the possession of a man who was at home, and insisted that he should sell it to me for use in the field. This he agreed to do, and the price was fixed at $125, for which I gave him an order on my father.

The coat being produced was found to be a large oil-cloth coat, the left sleeve of which had been split up on the inside, and also across the breast, and afterward sewed up, while just below the shoulder two bullet holes had been patched up, and at the end of the sleeve the course of another bullet had been repaired by turning down an additional hem.

As soon as I saw the coat I was struck by the well known fact that Stonewall Jackson had been wounded in exactly that way--two bullets in the left arm, and I remarked upon this coincidence.

Jones stated that he would not be surprised if it was General Jackson's coat, because the man who had brought it to him a day or two after the Battle of Chancellorsville had stated that he had gotten it from where General Jackson was wounded, and brought it away to sell, asking for it a peck of meal.

This charge Jones said he considered unreasonable, and had refused to pay it, as the coat was badly mutilated and very bloody, but that he had finally agreed to take it for a gallon of meal, which was accepted, and the coat was thrown into an old out house, along with a large amount of other plunder, blankets, knapsacks and such things as he had gathered from the battlefield. There it lay until the following fall, when, having to make a trip to Orange Courthouse in a spell of threatening weather, Mrs. Jones remembered this coat and repaired it so as to give her husband protection and satisfaction in a continuous and heavy rain.

I then opened the coat and examined it more carefully, and found in the inside of the back, in Jackson's own unmistakable handwriting, the name, "T.J. Jackson." I carried the coat home, but of course never pretended to use it. The only occasion thereafter on which it was used by any one was when it protected the venerable Commodore George N. Hollins, when he was driven from Charlottesville by Sheridan's cavalry, in March 1865. The coat remained at "Carysbrook" until in December 1867, when my father forwarded it to General R. E. Lee, at Lexington, Virginia, narrating the circumstances of his having gotten possession of it, and requesting him to make a proper disposition of so precious a relic. To this General Lee replied (I have his original letter) as follows:

>Lexington, Va., 13th December, 1867
>
>My Dear Sir, --I have received the overcoat worn by General T.J. Jackson at the time that he was wounded at the Wilderness. I am very much obliged to you for sending me so interesting a relic of one whose memory is so dear to me. Before making any disposition of it I think it proper to consult Mrs. Jackson, whose wishes on the subject are entitled to consideration.
>
>Mrs. Lee joins me in kindest regards to yourself and family, and I am very respectfully,
>Your obedient servant,
>R. E. LEE

♦ ♦ ♦

>Lexington Va., 18th January, 1868
>My Dear Sir: I informed you in December last that before making any disposition of the overcoat of General T. J. Jackson, I had written to Mrs. Jackson to ascertain her wishes on the subject. In a letter rec[eive]d from her this morning, she says: "Such a relic of my precious martyred husband would be extremely painful to

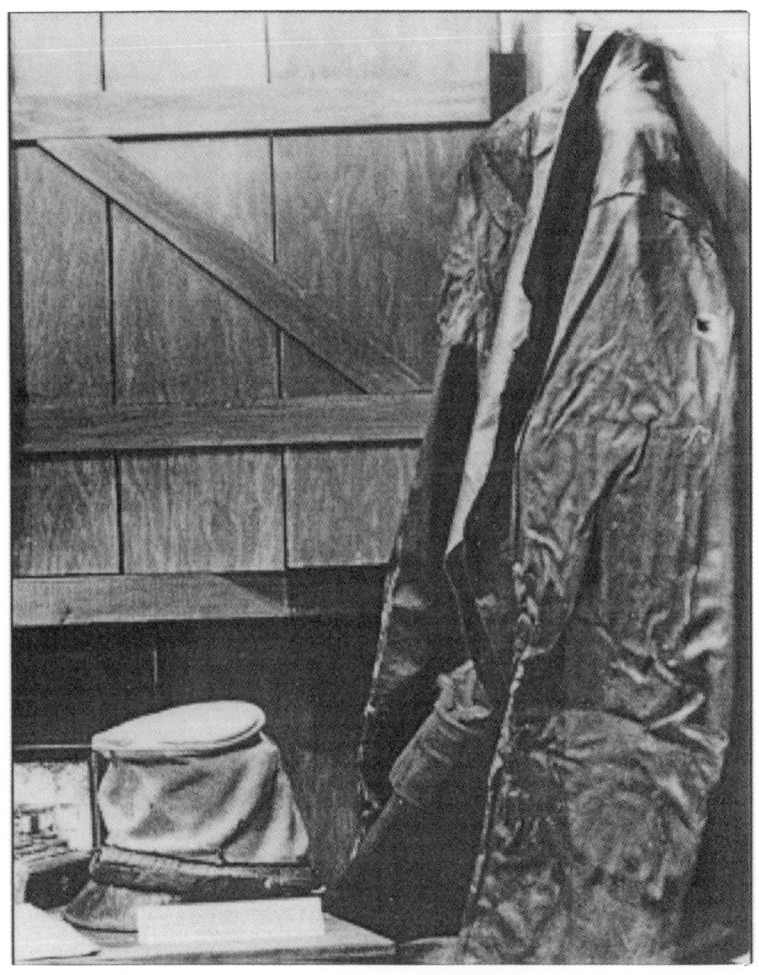

COURTESY VIRGINIA MILITARY INSTITUTE MUSEM
THE OILCLOTH COAT
On the right is the oilcloth coat Stonewall Jackson wore the evening he was wounded. Note the bullet hole in the upper left arm. This coat is on display at the Virginia Military Institute Museum along with Jackson's forage cap (shown at left).

me, and yet I cannot reconcile myself to think of its being in any other possession than my own."

I have, therefore, forwarded it to her with a copy of your letter, that she may see how it was recovered and to whom she is indebted for it.

Hoping that this disposition of a relic familiar to my eyes and painfully interesting to the hearts of all our people may receive your approbation, I am, with great respect, very truly yours,

R. E. LEE

It has been stated that this coat was obtained by some devoted Scotch admirers of General Jackson, and has been seen by American travelers . . . in a museum in Glasgow, Scotland. Whether this latter part is correct or not, I am unable to say. ♦

A POEM
BY
MARY ASHLEY TOWNSEND

This poem was written for the May 10, 1881, unveiling of a statue of Stonewall Jackson in a New Orleans cemetery--the statue surmounts a large tomb built for the soldiers who fought for Stonewall.

>Comrades, halt! The field is chosen.
>   'Neath the skies of Southern May,
>Where the Southern roses ripen,
>   We will bivouac to-day.
>Here no foe will draw our sabres
>   In the turbulence of war,
>Nor will drum beat, nor will bugle
>   Wake the old pain in a scar.
>
>All is rest, and calm--around us
>   Beauty's smile and manhood's prime;
>Scents of Spring, like ships, go sailing
>   Balmy seas of summer time.
>Flags of battle, hanging yonder,
>   Flutter not at strife's increase;
>On their pulses lie the fingers
>   Of the Great Physician--Peace.
>
>In the marble camp before us,
>   Silence paces to and fro--
>Spectre of the din of battles
>   Hard fought in the long ago.
>While he marches, from the meadows,
>   O'er the heights, around the curves;
>Come the men of many combats--
>   Death's Grand Army of Reserves.
>
>In the swift advancing columns,
>   Many a battle-blazoned name.
>With Stuart, Ewell, Hays and Ashby,
>   Bears the honor cross of Fame.
>Down the spectral line it flashes--
>   Glorious symbol of reward
>Won when all the world was looking
>   Unto Lee and Beauregard.

From the war-graves of Manassas,
    Fredericksburg and Malvern Hill;
Garrick's Ford and Massanutton,
    Fast the shadowy legions fill.
From the far off Rappahannock,
    From the red fields of Cross Keys,
Gettysburg--the Wildernesses--
    From defeats and victories:

Tired trooper--weary marcher--
    Grim and sturdy cannonier--
Veteran gray, and slender stripling,
    Hasten to encamp them here.
From the mountain and the river,
    From the city and the plain,
Sweeping down to join their leader--
    STONEWALL JACKSON--once again.

There he stands; alive in granite!
    By the hand of genius made
Once again to rise before us,
    Waiting for his "Old Brigade."
Chieftain--Hero--Christian--Soldier--
    King of men, and man of God!
Crystalized about his footsteps,
    Greatness marks the path he trod.

Soldiers! Ye who fought with Jackson
    Through the days and nights of strife;
Bringing from the fields of battle
    But the bitter lees of life:
Ye whose lips have only tasted
    Ashen apples from the fray;
Every wound ye won beside him,
    Knights ye on the field today

Army of our old Virginia!
    Would ye write a legend
That shall win from friend and foeman,
    Honors' reverential tear?
Trace ye then upon this marble,
    With imperishable pen,
Words that shout their own hozannas,
    STONEWALL JACKSON AND HIS MEN!

COURTESY SHORNE HARRISON
JULIA JACKSON
Julia and her mother Mary Anna took part in the ceremonies in New Orleans in May 1881 when a statue of Stonewall Jackson was dedicated there. This photograph was taken sometime during Julia's visit on this occasion. Pinned to her dress are souvenir badges given to her by Confederate veterans.

GOODBYE TO STONEWALL

BY

HENRY KYD DOUGLAS

PRIVATE, LIEUTENANT, AND CAPTAIN
COMPANY B, SECOND VIRGINIA REGIMENT
STONEWALL BRIGADE
AND LATER
MEMBER OF JACKSON'S STAFF

Henry Kyd Douglas, born in Shepherdstown, (now West) Virginia, September 29, 1840, was the youngest member of Stonewall Jackson's staff. He had graduated from college in Pennsylvania, studied law in Lexington, Virginia, been admitted to the bar, and begun to practice in St. Louis, Missouri, by the time the Civil War started. He immediately returned to Virginia and enlisted. After his service with the Second Virginia Regiment, Douglas served on Jackson's staff--as assistant inspector general and assistant adjutant general-- until Jackson's death. He then served on the staffs of several other Confederate generals, among them Jubal Early and John B. Gordon. Douglas was wounded several times and taken prisoner twice before the war was finally over for him; the second time he was imprisoned was after the surrender, when he was accused of "violation of parole," "violation of military orders" (wearing his gray uniform), and treason. He was found guilty of the second charge and "not guilty" of the others.

After the war Henry Kyd Douglas became a well known lawyer, especially in Maryland where he eventually settled. In addition to practicing law, he spent the years after the war writing about Jackson. He died of tuberculosis in Hagerstown, Maryland, in 1903.

. . . I was present at Lexington when the Jackson statue erected at his grave was unveiled. It was a day not to be forgotten. Old Confederates were there from far and near--men who had not see each other since Appomattox. The Valley of Virginia gathered there, and all the old soldiers in grey hair or grey beards, crowded the streets of that historic town. The day was given up to memories, and Jubal Early, the oldest Confederate general living, spoke for us all on that occasion. I need not dwell upon the ceremonies, upon the pathetic scenes at this last reunion. The evening drew near and the departing day seemed to linger like a benediction over the sacred place of the dead. People were moving off and the order was given to the old soldiers to fall in line and march away. With trembling step the grey line moved on, but when it reached the gate one old Confederate turned his face for a last look at the monument and, waving his old grey hat toward the figure of his beloved General, he cried out in a voice, that choked itself with sobs,

"Good-by, old man, good-by! We've done all we can for you!" ♦

"OUR STONEWALL"
Stonewall Jackson Cemetery in Lexington, Virginia

COURTESY MARIAN NOVAK

A SHRINE IN THE VALLEY
BY
DR. HUNTER HOLMES MCGUIRE

The words below were spoken by Dr. Hunter McGuire at Stonewall Jackson's grave in Lexington, Virginia, July 21, 1891, 30 years after the Battle of First Manassas, when the statue of Stonewall by Valentine was unveiled there.

And so I leave the grave of my general and my friend, knowing that for centuries men will come to Lexington as a Mecca, and to this grave as a Shrine, and wonderingly talk of this man and his mighty deeds. I know that time will only add to his great fame. I know that his name will be honored and revered forever, just as I know that the beautiful river, flowing near by, will sing an unceasing requiem to his memory--just as I know that the proud mountains, like some vast chain of sentinels, will keep eternal watch over his honored grave. ♦

SUGGESTED BIBLIOGRAPHY

Complete bibliographic information for works used follows the first citation of each in the endnotes (beginning on page 191). The reader new to the subject of Stonewall Jackson and interested in learning more can turn to numerous biographies, including those published during his life, those published within a few years of his death, and those published very recently. The following significant works (a mere few of those available) are a good beginning. (They are listed in chronological rather than the usual alphabetical order):

Dabney, Robert Lewis. LIFE AND CAMPAIGNS OF LIEUT.-GEN. THOMAS J. JACKSON (STONEWALL JACKSON). Richmond: Blelock, 1866. A full treatment of the Christian soldier by Reverend Dabney, who served on Jackson's staff.

Henderson, George Francis Robert. STONEWALL JACKSON AND THE AMERICAN CIVIL WAR (in two volumes). London: Longmans, Green, and Co., 1898. A more complete discussion than Dabney's (Henderson had access to official records).

Chambers, Lenoir. STONEWALL JACKSON (in two volumes). Wilmington, North Carolina: Broadfoot Publishing Company, 1988 (reprint of 1959 William Morrow edition). For the most part, a dependable and highly readable account of Jackson's life.

Robertson, James I., Jr. STONEWALL JACKSON: THE MAN, THE SOLDIER, THE LEGEND. New York: Macmillan Publishing USA, 1997. A thorough (160 pages of sources and notes alone--in tiny print!) study in which Robertson corrects misinformation and challenges assumptions found in earlier biographies.

There are of course many, many other sources, and the reader wanting a fuller bibliography can turn to such lists as the short-title index in Chambers and the (truly exhaustive) bibliography in Robertson (both listed above). If the interest is in Stonewall's men, an excellent beginning is:

Robertson, James I., Jr. THE STONEWALL BRIGADE. Baton Rouge: Louisiana State University Press, 1963.

ENDNOTES

INTRODUCTION

Cover: The *carte de visite* featured on the front cover is from one of only two photographs taken of Stonewall Jackson during the Civil War, this one made in April 1863--only days before his death--at the Yerby House near Fredericksburg by Mr. D.T. Cowell of the Minnis Gallery of Richmond. Like other photographs of Stonewall, it was later widely distributed as a *carte de visite*. A *carte de visite* was a kind of thin-cardboard "visiting card" about 2" x 3", which featured a photograph-portrait, this portrait sometimes printed on thin paper and pasted to the cardboard; often the name and address of the photographer or producer of these *cartes de visite* were printed on the back. Such cards became very popular in North America during the Civil War among the general populace of both North and South, including among the soldiers, their families and friends. They were inexpensive photographs of loved ones and an inexpensive method of obtaining photographs of admired and well-known personalities such as Stonewall. **Page ii--Frontispiece**: This portrait of Stonewall was painted by Louis Mattieu Didier Guillaume and presented to the Virginia Military Institute in Lexington, Virginia, by Meriwether Jones, class of 1874. It now hangs in the Jackson Memorial Hall on the VMI campus and is reproduced here for the first time. **Page v--Dedication Page**: "A Federal Soldier" is quoted from *Southern Historical Society Papers*, X (1882), p. 334; **Page vi**: THE CIVIL WAR: LEE TAKES COMMAND (Alexandria, Virginia: Time-Life Books, 1985), p. 63. **Page xviii**: Photograph of area near Lexington is from Mary Anna Jackson's LIFE AND LETTERS OF STONEWALL JACKSON--hereafter LIFE AND LETTERS (New York, New York: Harper Brothers, 1892), p. 52; copies of many letters written by Jackson can be found in the Virginia Military Institute (VMI) Archives in Lexington, Virginia, the one to Laura quoted here being one of them. **Page xxii**: Drawing of the Jackson home from LIFE AND LETTERS (see endnote for page xviii above), p. 107. **Page xxiii**: Map is from John Esten Cooke, STONEWALL JACKSON: A MILITARY BIOGRAPHY (New York: D. Appleton and Company, 1876), p. 76. **Page xxvi**: Photograph of Redwood is from Francis T. Miller, THE PHOTOGRAPHIC HISTORY OF THE CIVIL WAR IN TEN VOLUMES (New York: Review of Reviews Company, 1912), X, p. 27 (hereafter "Miller"). **Page xxvii**: Much of Redwood's bibliographic material is from notes, letters, and documents located in his files in the Museum of the Confederacy in Richmond, Virginia. **Page xxxi**: General Johnson's words ("You are the last drawer. . . .") are from an April 6, 1910, letter he wrote to Redwood, now at the Museum of the Confederacy in Richmond. **Page xxxiii**: Confederate General Zebulon Vance is also buried in this cemetery, and there is a marker to guide the tourist to his grave. **Page xxxv**: From James A. Walker in *Southern Historical Society Papers*, XX (1892), pp. 372-374; bibliographic information about Walker can be found in Willie Walker Caldwell, STONEWALL JIM (Elliston, Virginia: Northcross House, 1990); although there were survivors of the Stonewall Brigade, the unit was so badly reduced in numbers that its members were combined with other surviving members of (John Marshall) Jones' and (George H.) Steuart's

Brigades to form (William) Terry's Brigade, and as such surrendered at Appomattox (James I. Robertson, Jr., THE STONEWALL BRIGADE [Baton Rouge: Louisiana State University Press, 1991], p. 226). **Page xxxviii**: The quotation below the photograph is from p. 16 of John Newton Lyle's, "Stonewall Jackson's Guard," a typescript located in Special Collections, Leyburn Library, Washington and Lee University in Lexington, Virginia, used by permission, and hereafter referred to as "Lyle."

PART I

Page 4: This photograph is from G.F.R. Henderson, STONEWALL JACKSON AND THE CIVIL WAR--in two volumes and hereafter "Henderson"--(New York: Longmans, Green, and Co., 1905), I, p. 54. **Page 6**: The artist and date of this romantic portrait of Elinor Junkin Jackson are unknown. It is difficult to say whether or not it provides a good likeness. The one existing photograph of Elinor shows a plainer and more somber woman; and yet the basic features of the subjects of both photograph and painting are very similar. Having to sit motionless (and thus "smileless") several minutes for the picture-taking process then in use robbed many an otherwise attractive face of its charm; the photograph of Jackson was probably taken by Matthew Brady in New York in 1851--according to researchers, it was "apparently retrieved from" his files after Jackson became popular in the Civil War (p. 1 of "More than an Image: A Portrait of Stonewall Jackson by William Carl Browne," unpub. paper by Jeffrey L. Ball, August 18, 1988, in the Special Collections, Leyburn Library, Washington and Lee University). **Pages 5-7**: The quotation beginning at the bottom of page 5 herein and ending at the top of page 7 is from Lyle (see endnote for page xxxviii above), p. 14. **Page 7**: The quotation beginning "[h]e . . . outlived every prejudice. . . ." is from A SURGEON WITH STONEWALL JACKSON: THE CIVIL WAR LETTERS OF DR. HARVEY BLACK, ed. by Glenn L. McMullen (Baltimore: Butternut and Blue, 1995), p. 50--letter of May 10, 1863, to his wife; "greatest and noblest in that. . ." is from James Power Smith," *Battles and Leaders of the Civil War*, III (1888), p. 214. **Page 8**: Like Elinor's, the portrait of Mary Anna Jackson presents a mystery: its creator, and present owner and location are unknown--it is believed, however, that it was painted about the time of her marriage to Thomas Jackson in 1857; the caption is from Lyle (see endnote for page xxxviii above), p. 226. **Page 9**: This engraving of Jackson is after one of the poses from what is called the "Winchester photograph" (see page xxxvii herein). **Page 10**: Michael Miley was a Lexington photographer whose photographs of Lexington and its population are much prized today as historical documentation. **Page 11**: Information about John Newton Lyle (see endnote for page xxxviii above) is from his files in Special Collections, Leyburn Library, Washington and Lee University in Lexington, Virginia; this piece is from Lyle, p. 16. **Page 13**: Bibliographic information about VMI graduates of the period can be found in Charles D. Walker, BIBLIOGRAPHICAL SKETCHES OF THE GRADUATES AND ELEVES OF THE VIRGINIA MILITARY INSTITUTE (Philadelphia: J.B. Lippincott & Co., 1875) and in files in the Virginia Military Institute Archives--this information on Obenchain is from his files at the VMI Archives; this piece is from *Southern Historical Society Papers*, XVI (1888), pp. 44-47; on p. 46 of his article, the page on which Obenchain quotes Jackson's speech, the author notes: "This speech is quoted from memory, after a lapse of twenty-five years. It made so deep an impression at the time that the writer believes he has given the first and last parts in Jackson's own words. The other part may vary somewhat in language, but it is the same in substance"; the quotation beginning "One afternoon . . ." is from Edward Moore, STORY OF A CANNONEER UNDER STONEWALL JACKSON (New York: the Neale Publishing Company, 1907), pp. 20-21. **Page 15**: Jackson's way of saying the word "oblique" was the correct military and nautical pronunciation. **Page 16**: "But the fact is, Jackson had one way of saying things. . . ."--the fact is, Jackson memorized his lectures word for word. Regarding the quotation that ends with the claim that Jackson never "seem[ed] the least annoyed," one exception on record is Jackson's reaction to the classroom behavior (at VMI) of the hot-tempered young cadet James Alexander Walker, whom he had arrested (see page xxxv herein). **Page 20**: The photograph is from the Sidney Briggs Collection at the VMI Archives; McGuire's quotation is from *Southern Historical Society Papers*, XVI (1889), p. 47. **Page 21**: Bibliographic information on George Moffett is from Richard L. Armstrong, 11TH VIRGINIA CAVALRY (Lynchburg, Virginia: H.E. Howard, Co., 1989), p. 168; Moffett's piece is from *Southern Historical Society Papers*, XXII (1894), pp. 155-156. **Page 22**: The actual number of cadets is given as 176 in Lenoir Chambers' two-volume work, STONEWALL JACKSON (Wilmington, North Carolina: Broadfoot Publishing Company, 1988), I, p. 6 (hereafter "Chambers"); the exact hour of departure is disputed: "high noon," 12:30 PM (James I. Robertson, Jr., STONEWALL JACKSON: THE MAN, THE SOLDIER, THE LEGEND [New York: Macmillan Publishing USA, 1997], p. 824), and 1:00 PM (Chambers [see note for page 22 above], I, p. 310), who says that the cadets were "formed to march" at 12:30 and that "the hour of [actual] movement" was set at 1:00 PM; the actual command, "Jackson's first command of the Civil War," according to Chambers (I, p. 3 [see endnote for page 22 above]) was: "'Right face! By the file left, march! By the file left, march!'"; Lyle's piece is from Lyle (see endnote for page xxxviii above), p. 55. **Page 23**: The information in the caption is from Chambers (see endnote for page 22 above), Vol II, p. 274. **Page 24**: Brady apparently modified his 1851 negative plate of this photograph (see endnote for page 6 above) to make Jackson's image "current" by adding officer's insignia.

PART II

Page 27: McGuire, *Southern Historical Society Papers*, XIX (1891), pp. 301-315, *passim*. **Page 32**: The "servant" referred to here was very probably Jim Lewis, about whom little is known except that he was a black man from Lexington who served Jackson well and after Jackson Sandie Pendleton, soon after whose death in the war Jim Lewis himself sickened and died; it is even uncertain as to whether he was a slave or a "freedman." It is certain that he was not one of Jackson's slaves, so if he was not free, he was possibly hired from his unknown owner. Jackson owned six slaves--three of whom he bought and three of whom were brought to the marriage by Mary Anna. Albert, Jackson's first slave, had asked Jackson to purchase him so that he in turn could purchase his own freedom from

Jackson (this was apparently accomplished by Albert's working at such establishments as the various hotels in town); Amy, who became the Jacksons' cook, was a middle-aged woman who was to be auctioned off and, like Albert, asked Jackson to buy her; and finally a young (four-year-old) orphan named Emma, who had learning difficulties and whose owner was an elderly widow who seemingly wanted to place the little girl well, came into the Jackson household (where she was--according to Anna--never really "useful"). Those slaves in the household who came with Mary Anna were her former nurse Hetty, who had the general responsibility of running the household, and Hetty's two teenaged sons. Moses Drury Hoge was the pastor of the Second Presbyterian Church in Richmond (Jackson often fell asleep in church--in spite of sitting "bolt upright"). **Page 33**: The Yerby House, called "Belvoir," was the home of Thomas Yerby and was located about two miles south of Jackson's (temporary) headquarters at Hamilton's Crossing near Fredericksburg. General Maxy Gregg died in this house, and in April 1863 Jackson's wife Mary Anna and baby Julia visited Jackson here--the first time the new father had seen his five-month-old child--and Julia was baptized in the Yerbys' parlor on April 23, 1863. Little Julia and her mother stayed at Belvoir until April 29, 1863, when the guns of war began to fire again. Less than two weeks later Stonewall was dead. **Page 34**: This was General Reuban Lindsay Walker; on December 23, 1862, Ted Barclay (see page 145 herein) wrote home about this incident at Dam No. 5:

"Jack [Stonewall] detailed men from each company, did not happen to get your humble servant, [sent] the detachment towards dam number 5 which, by the way, is the main dam on the river [the Chesapeake and Ohio Canal]. Getting opposite the dam they were told to lie close and dodge Yankee bullets. After a while crowbars, axes, picks and shovels without number were piled up on the bank and a barrel of whiskey. Old Jack gave each man a tinful and took some himself and told them to pitch into the dam and tear it down" (Charles W. Turner, LETTERS FROM THE STONEWALL BRIGADE [Natural Bridge Station, Virginia: Rockbridge Publishing Company, 1992], p. 37).

Page 36-38: These final two sections by McGuire are from *Southern Historical Society Papers*, XXV (1897), the first found on p. 97 and the second on p. 107. **Page 36:** "I was utterly overcome..."--McGuire was very emotional about leaving Winchester because not only was he a native, but also his parents and siblings were still residents of the town; the "fine lad" described here was William C. "Willie" Preston, the stepson of Jackson's dear friend (and sister of his first wife) Maggie Preston and son of his close friend and companion (and founder of VMI) Colonel John T.L. Preston. **Page 38:** The "lad we all loved" was Willie Preston. **Page 39**: From Lyle (see endnote for page xxxviii above), pp. 95-96. **Page 41**: "... [A]bout two o'clock..." from LIFE AND LETTERS, p. 175; "After pacing around the camp..." from LIFE AND LETTERS, pp. 175-176. **Page 42**: Amanda Edmonds' diary entries are from JOURNALS OF AMANDA VIRGINIA EDMONDS: LASS OF THE MOSBY CONFEDERACY 1859-1867, ed. by Nancy Chappelear Baird (Stephens City, Virginia: Commercial Press, 1984), pp. 53-54; Preston's speech is found on p. 1 of the *Lexington Gazette*. **Page 42-43**: "... Ashby's Gap swallowed us..." from Lyle (see endnote for page xxxviii above), pp. 180-181. **Page 46**: Benjamin Franklin Reinhart was born in Pennsylvania in 1844; he studied art in New York, Germany, and Paris, and in 1861 traveled to England where he stayed seven years. It was during this time that he painted this portrait of Jackson, presumably relying on a *carte de visite* from the modified 1851 Brady photograph (see page 24 herein and endnote above), and perhaps contemporaneous eye-witness descriptions by such people as the Englishman Viscount Wolseley (see page 125 herein). Reinhart died in 1896. This is a rare reproduction, perhaps the first, of this portrait of Stonewall.

PART III

Page 48: This map is from Henderson (see endnote for page 4 above), I, p. 142.
Page 50: Robins' piece is from *Southern Historical Society Papers*, XIX (1891), pp. 166-167. **Page 51**: This "equestrian statue" is by Joseph Pollia and was dedicated August 31, 1940; the caption is from Lyle (see endnote for page xxxviii above), p. 96. **Page 52**: This piece is from Lyle, p. 7; the *Lexington Gazette* (May 27, 1861) called the LHV a "handsome and well-drilled company"; for a history of the Stonewall Brigade, see James I. Robertson, Jr., THE STONEWALL BRIGADE (Baton Rouge; Louisiana State University Press, 1963 or 1991). **Page 53**: The man who drew this sketch, Dr. Adelbert J. Volck, was a dentist from Baltimore who, it is said, drew this portrait of Stonewall "from life" (Roy Bird Cook, THE FAMILY AND EARLY LIFE OF STONEWALL JACKSON, fifth edition [Charleston, West Virginia: Education Foundation, Inc., 1967], p. 188; the caption is from Lyle (see endnote for page xxxviii above), p. 6. **Page 54**: This piece is from p. 67 of CULLINGS FROM THE CONFEDERACY, compiled by Nora Fontaine M. Davidson (Washington, D.C.: The Rufus H. Darby Printing Company, 1903). **Page 55**: This piece is from p. 167 of MEMOIRS OF LIFE IN AND OUT OF THE ARMY IN VIRGINIA DURING THE WAR BETWEEN THE STATES, compiled by Susan Leigh Blackford and annotated and edited by Charles Minor Blackford, in two volumes, originally published in 1894 by J.P. Bell Printers of Lynchburg, Virginia, "exclusively for the private use of their family," and reprinted in 1996 by Warwick Publishing Company of the same city. The Blackford material is interesting and important, but researchers should be aware that the published "letters," while based on actual family letters (in the Jones Memorial Library in Lynchburg), have been augmented and otherwise edited by Charles M. Blackford so that information ascribed to a particular letter is often not found in the original letter of that date and is in fact sometimes significantly changed. A later edition by a grandson, Charles M. Blackford III (LETTERS FROM LEE'S ARMY [New York: Charles Scribner's Sons, 1947]) is even further deranged, making the Warwick edition the best available, since the original letters have never been published. **Page 56**: Background information and letter are from Roy Bird Cook, pp. 188-189. **Page 57**: The sketch (on left) of Jackson reclining is from the Alexander Galt diary, 1861-1862, Galt Family Papers, Manuscripts and Rare Books Department, Swem Library, College of William and Mary, Williamsburg, Virginia, and is used here by permission; the pencil sketch of Stonewall by Boteler (on right) was found inserted in a copy of the original

printing of some of the material written by John Esten Cooke for the *Southern Illustrated News* which went into a collection of his articles called STONEWALL JACKSON AND THE OLD STONEWALL BRIGADE--the sketch is now at the Tracy W. McGregor Library, Special Collections Department, University of Virginia Library, Charlottesville, Virginia, and is used by permission; the original articles which Cooke wrote for the *Southern Illustrated News* (he became their correspondent in January 1863) were later collected, reprinted, and published (edited by Richard Harwell) in 1954 by the University of Virginia Press at Charlottesville (the sketch is following p. 16 of this 1954 collection). **Page 58**: Background information and letters from Dr. William S. White, SKETCHES FROM THE LIFE OF CAPTAIN HUGH A. WHITE OF THE STONEWALL BRIGADE (Columbia, South Carolina: South Carolina Steam Press, 1864), p. 61. **Page 59**: Caption from Lyle (see endnote for page xxxviii above), p. 11. **Page 60**: Information and quotation below illustration of the first national flag ("Stars and Bars") are from Joseph H. Crute, Jr., EMBLEMS OF SOUTHERN VALOR (Louisville, Kentucky: Harmony House, 1990), p. 13. Redwood writes of the Southern soldier's relationship to the various flags used by the South during the Civil War (three national flags and one battle flag):

> "As to devotion to his flag, he had scarcely time to cultivate the sentiment which figured so largely in the patriotic fervor of his opponents. No one of the 'motley many' national ensigns ever entirely received his approval. . . . He did, in time, come to develop respect and affection for his battle-flag . . . mainly as a convenient object upon which to dress up a line of battle or to serve as a rallying-point in the event of that line being broken" (Miller [see endnote for page xxvi above], VIII, pp. 152-154).

Page 61: In the last century lemons were an imported luxury in the Shenandoah Valley where Jackson lived from 1851-1861, so there is no record of Jackson's discussing this fruit as a personal or local crop, as he did other fruit. Recipes in 19th-century American cookbooks frequently mention lemons--and ways to preserve them, since before refrigeration they could be transported successfully from their warm-weather sources only during the cold months of the year--so it is rather certain Jackson had "experienced" them before the war. During the Civil War the Union tried to keep its army, especially the Medical Department, supplied with lemons; lemonade was considered a primary medicinal drink, for by tradition it was "recommended to clarify the blood and ease sick stomach" (William J. Darby *et al*, food: THE GIFT OF OSIRIS [London: Academic Press, 1977], p. 705). It is possible that Jackson's taste for the fruit was developed during the war, when "Yankee spoil" made the fruit available--that Mary Anna did not seem to know how to mix lemonade for her husband seems to point in this direction, though she may well have been too distraught to remember. (At one point as Jackson lay dying Mary Anna was kept busy making lemonade for him. When his aide James Power Smith, who was occasionally in charge of Jackson's "mess," brought the drink to the general, Stonewall said, "You did not make this. It is too sweet. Take it back" [Chambers (see endnote for page 22 above), II, p. 440]). Three contemporaries describe Jackson eating a lemon during the Civil War: General Richard Taylor (Richard B. Harwell, ed., DESTRUCTION AND RECONSTRUCTION [New York: Longmans, Green, and Co., 1955], p. 51-52), has the general sitting on a fence while eating the lemon and adds, "Where Jackson got his lemons, 'no fellow could find out,' but he was rarely without one"; John Esten Cooke, in STONEWALL JACKSON AND THE OLD . . . BRIGADE (see endnote for page 57 above), p. 10, writes, "Moving about slowly and sucking a lemon (Yankee spoil, no doubt) the celebrated General Stonewall looked as little like a general as possible" (Cooke wrote this piece while a war correspondent for the *Southern Illustrated News* and it was published while Jackson was still alive [in February 1863]); and Henry Kyd Douglas (I RODE WITH STONEWALL [no place: Fawcett Publications, 1961], p. 108) writes:

> "General Jackson . . . moved to the front [at Cold Harbor]. At that moment someone handed him a lemon--a fruit of which he was especially fond. Immediately a small piece was bitten out of it and slowly and unsparingly he began to extract its flavor and its juice. From that moment until darkness ended the battle, that lemon scarcely left his lips. . . ."

(Though sometimes dismissed and derided for its imprecision, especially regarding events at which Douglas was not present, I RODE WITH STONEWALL is nevertheless an interesting and compelling memoir featuring Stonewall Jackson); this piece is from Lyle (see endnote for page xxxviii above), p. 309. **Page 62**: "[Quartermaster] Harman tried to resign several times, and his letters to his brother in Staunton are one long tale of woe as a quartermaster under Jackson" (Chambers [see endnote for page 22 above], I, p. 335); that Jackson would "have a man shot . . ." is from Sam R. Watkins, "CO. AYTCH" (Wilmington, North Carolina: Broadfoot Publishing Company, 1990), p. 60; "Jackson is considered rigid . . . " from Captain James White, OLD ZEUS, ed. by Charles W. Turner (Verona, Virginia: McClure Press, 1983), p. 43; "General Jackson is rigid . . . although not more so . . ." from OLD ZEUS, p. 78; "Man that is born of woman . . ." from Royall W. Figg, WHERE MEN ONLY DARE TO GO: STORY OF A BOY COMPANY (Richmond, Virginia: Whittet and Shepperson, 1885), p. 64; about this march to Romney Colonel Tailiaferro said, "The best army I ever saw of its strength has been destroyed by . . . bad marching and bad management" (Chambers [see endnote for page 22 above], I, p. 430); a soldier said the troops

> "were out nearly one month, and had miserable weather all the time. . . . We lost more men from sickness than if we had been engaged in a big battle. We accomplished nothing. . . . Winchester was full of soldiers sick with pneumonia, and they died by the hundreds" (Robert Gaither Tanner, STONEWALL IN THE VALLEY [Garden City, New York: Doubleday, 1976], p. 82);

"Our confidence in our leader . . ." from William Poague, GUNNER WITH STONEWALL (Jackson, Tennessee: McCownt-Mercer Press, 1957), p. 18. **Page 63**: "One secret of Stonewall's success . . ." Sam Watkins, p. 60; the first section of Sam Watkin's piece is from p. 56 of his book and the second from pp. 56-57. **Page 65**: This piece is from Miller (see endnote for page xxvi above), X, pp. 98-116; Jackson resigned at this point in essence because he had been passed over in the chain of command--a civilian authority attempted to issue an order affecting one of Jackson's subordinates, and as the commander in the field, Jackson felt he had no option but to resist by tendering his resignation. **Page 73**: Regarding the quotation beginning "never a showy horseman," not only was Jackson not "showy" on a horse, he was often ridiculed for his riding ability by troops more accustomed to the very upright, stiff military riding style more usual for officers. And yet he was a good horseman, having been trained by his Uncle Cummins to race horses. One anonymous writer, an "expert" on horsemanship, noted the following in 1876:

> "Lieutenant-General Thomas Jonathan ("Stonewall") Jackson was a great horseman. He sat in the saddle easily, while there was a sort of abandon visible which showed his familiarity with horseflesh from boyhood. His seat was very erect, and though it had none of the stiffness of the cavalry style, it was very correct. His stirrups were shortened to give a slight bend to the knee and enable him to adjust his body to the movements of his steed without apparent exertion" (*Southern Historical Society Papers*, II [1876], p. 173).

Page 77: From Andrew Davidson Long, STONEWALL'S FOOT CAVALRYMAN, ed. by Dr. Walter E. Long (Austin, Texas, 1965), pp. 11-14. Privately printed and used by the gracious permission of Mrs. Walter E. Long. **Pages 78-79**: This map of the Valley is from Henderson (see endnote for page 4 above), I, p. 214. **Page 81**: The map is by Jackson's famous mapmaker Jed Hotchkiss and is from Henderson (see endnote for page 4 above), I, p. 340. **Page 83**: This piece is reprinted from William H. Andrews, FOOTPRINTS OF A REGIMENT: A RECOLLECTION OF THE GEORGIA REGULARS (Atlanta: Longstreet Press, 1992), pp. 48-49. **Page 86**: The background information and piece are from Henry Marvin Wharton, WAR SONGS AND POEMS (Philadelphia: John C. Winston Company, 1904), pp. 8-9. **Page 88**: From MEMOIRS OF LIFE IN AND OUT OF THE ARMY IN VIRGINIA . . . (see endnote for page 55 above), p. 180. **Page 89**: In all likelihood Stonewall would not have approved of Blackford's helping the Union officer escape. Shortly after the incident Blackford writes about in this letter, another took place which attests to this. On September 14, 1862, at South Mountain, the Fifth Alabama, Rodes' Brigade, commanded by a Major Hobson, was trying to "prevent a flank movement by the enemy" who was being led and urged on by a very brave officer on a white horse. Major Hobson selected a rifleman to "pick him off," and once that was done, the Confederates were able to stop the Federals:

> "Subsequently, and not long before the battle of Sharpsburg . . . an officer from General Jackson came to [Major Hobson] with the 'compliments of General Jackson' and the message: 'Tell Major Hobson I want the brave officers of the enemy killed off. Their death insures our success. Cowards are never in front; they skulk or flee!'" (*Southern Historical Society Papers*, XXV [1897], p. 105).

It is telling that Blackford's original letter (in the Jones Memorial Library at Lynchburg) contains only the "outline" of this incident and does not mention that Blackford allowed the Union officer to escape--an action which might have been much frowned upon during the war, and the discussion of which in a letter might have been risky. **Page 90**: Information about this song is from John Esten Cooke, p. 16 (see endnote for page 4 above); lyrics are from WAR SONGS AND POEMS (see endnote for page 86 above), pp. 44-48. **Page 92**: The portions of this article printed in italics are from "With Stonewall Jackson," *Scribner's Monthly*, No. 18, pp.

220-233; those in regular type are from "With Jackson's 'Foot-Cavalry' at the Second Manassas," *Century Magazine*, No. 9, pp. 614-621. **Page 94**: The caption for this illustration is from D.H. Hill, "Lee Attacks North of the Chickahominy," *Battles and Leaders of the Civil War*, I (1884), p. 359. **Page 99**: The map of Cedar Mountain is from Henderson (see endnote for page 4 above), II, p. 96. **Page 117**: The quotation in the caption is from the *Lexington Gazette*, November 6, 1862, p. 1. **Page 118**: Information for the introduction is from BERRY BENSON'S CIVIL WAR BOOK: MEMOIRS OF A CONFEDERATE SHARPSHOOTER, ed. by Susan Williams Benson (Athens, Georgia: University of Georgia Press, 1991-1992), pp. xv-xvii; the text is from pp. 39-40 of same; the "B.& O.R.R." was the Baltimore and Ohio Rail Road. **Page 119**: General William Henry T. Walker, from South Carolina, and General T.R.R. Cobb, from Georgia, grace the back corners of this statue. **Page 121**: For a discussion of Jackson's nicknames, see Chambers (see endnote for page 22 above), I, pp. 237-238; background information and letter (written near Winchester, Virginia, October 1, 1862) are from Aurelia Austin, GEORGIA BOYS WITH "STONEWALL: JACKSON (Athens, Georgia: University of Georgia Press, 1967), p. 52. **Page 122**: The handsome and daring Kentuckian CSA General John Hunt Morgan was the leader of Morgan's Raiders. After "taring up Kentucki," Morgan was captured by the Union. He managed to escape, only to be trapped and shot down on September 4, 1864. **Page 123**: Map of Maryland from Henderson (see endnote for page 4 above), II, p. 240. **Page 124**: From Edward A. Pollard, SOUTHERN HISTORY OF THE WAR (New York: The Fairfax Press, 1866), p. 612, footnote. **Page 125**: Information in the introduction is from "A Month's Visit to the Confederate Headquarters," *Blackwood's Edinburgh Magazine*, January 1866, English edition LXIII (63), American edition LVI (56), pp. 1-29; the text is from p. 21. **Page 126**: This newspaper portrait of Jackson appeared December 6, 1862, and was probably drawn by Frank Vizetelly, an artist and correspondent for *The Illustrated London News*. This depiction complies with Wolseley's description, but is clearly drawn after the 1851 Brady photograph (see page 24 herein and note that the same collar insignia--with US shield--appear in both portraits). **Page 128**: Woodcut and caption are from the February 13, 1863, edition of the *News*, p. 185. **Page 132**: Biographical information is from Walter A. Montgomery, THE DAYS OF OLD AND THE YEARS THAT ARE PAST, privately printed, no place, no date; text is from pp. 33-34. **Page 133**: The Drecke letter (quoted at bottom) is in the Virginia Military Institute Archives. **Pages 134-135**: The map is from Henderson (see endnote for page 4 above), II, p. 468. **Page 136**: The text is from David Eldred Holt, A MISSISSIPPI REBEL IN THE ARMY OF NORTHERN VIRGINIA , ed. by Thomas D. Cockrell and Michael B. Ballard (Baton Rouge: Louisiana State University Press, 1955), p. 162. **Page 137**: The text is from Long (see endnote for page 77 above), pp. 15-16. **Page 139**: From *Battles and Leaders of the Civil War*, III (1888), pp. 204-205. **Page 140**: The Sheppard illustration is from p. 204 of Smith's article (see endnote for page 7 above). **Page 142**: The quotation in the introduction is from Chambers (see endnote for page 22 above), I, p. 380; the text is from Miller (see endnote for page xxvi above), X, pp. 114-115. **Page 143**: *The Last Meeting of Lee and Jackson* (originally called *Heroes of Chancellorsville*) was painted by Everett B.D. Julio, the son of an Italian mother and a Scottish father. He arrived in America just in time to witness the Civil War, settling first in the North and later

going South in search of a better climate. He settled in Louisiana and opened a studio in New Orleans where he painted *The Last Meeting* (dated 1869) and later an exact copy for Colonel D.F. Boyd, who donated it to Louisiana State University at Baton Rouge, where it hung until the mid-1980's, when it was cut from its frame and taken away by thieves. The original in its magnificent frame was eventually purchased from private hands by the Museum of the Confederacy in Richmond, Virginia, where it is on display. **Page 144**: The text is from *Southern Historical Society Papers*, XXV (1879), p. 110; General Fitzhugh Lee was Robert E. Lee's nephew; General Robert E. Rodes commanded a division under Jackson; he was from Lynchburg, a graduate of VMI, and admired by Jackson, who, as he lay dying at Guinea Station, commended Rodes for his gallantry at Chancellorsville. **Page 145**: Biographical information on Ted Barclay can be found in his files in the Special Collections of the Leyburn Library at Washington and Lee University in Lexington, the source also of the letter cited here. **Page 151**: The engraving on the preceding page and the introduction and poem on this page are from WAR SONGS AND POEMS, pp. 57-58. From the *Lexington Gazette*, May 20, 1863, p. 3, is this:
"As [Jackson] was being carried from the field, frequent enquiries was [sic] made by the soldiers, 'Who have you there?' He told the Doctor, 'Do not tell the troops that I am wounded.'"
Page 152: Captain Joseph Graham Morrison was Mary Anna's younger brother (and so Jackson's brother-in-law) and a cadet on leave from VMI when he joined Jackson's staff. **Page 153**: From Berry Benson (see endnote for page 118 above), pp. 39-40; the quotation at the bottom of the page is from the December 1863 ANNUAL REPORT (Augusta, Maine: Stevens & Sayward, 1863), p. 124. **Page 154**: From a letter in the Virginia Military Institute Archives. **Page 159**: Barclay letter is in the Special Collections, Leyburn Library, Washington and Lee University. **Page 161**: From John O. Casler, FOUR YEARS IN THE STONEWALL BRIGADE (Girard, Kansas: Appeal Publishing Company, 1906) second edition, pp. 153-158. **Page 163**: About the men of the Stonewall Brigade not being allowed to accompany Jackson's body, Henry Kyd Douglas wrote the following:

"On Monday, at the request of the officers of the Stonewall Brigade, I went to ask General Lee if in his judgment it was proper to permit that brigade or a part of it to escort the remains of General Jackson to Richmond. He received me kindly, listened patiently, and then in a voice gentle and sad replied: 'I am sure no one can feel the loss of General Jackson more deeply than I do, for no one has the same reason. I can appreciate the feelings of his old brigade; they have reason to mourn for him, for he was proud of them . . . I am sorry the situation of affairs will not justify me in letting them go to Richmond or even to Lexington. But it cannot be. Those people over the river are again showing signs of movement and I cannot leave my Headquarters long enough to ride to the depot and pay my dear friend the poor tribute of seeing his body placed upon the cars. . . . [General Jackson] never neglected a duty while living and would not rest easier in his grave if his old brigade left the presence of the enemy to see him buried" (I RODE WITH STONEWALL [see endnote for page 61 above]). **Page 169**: The biographical information and letter quoted are from the file of Samuel Baldwin Hannah at the Virginia Military Institute Archives, Lexington, Virginia. **Page 171:** This is a very rare photograph of VMI cadets at Jackson's grave. **Page 172**: The biographical information and diary entries are from the file of Charles Thomas Haigh at the Virginia Military Institute Archives. **Page 174**: This well-known engraving is by Civil War correspondent and artist Thomas Nast, who has taken Jackson's likeness from the last photograph of him, added a body and a camp background. **Page 176**: Redwood's text is from Miller (see endnote for page xxvi above), X, p. 116. **Page 177**: Walter Montgomery (see endnote for page 132 above), pp. 60-61. **Page 178**: This article first appeared in the *Richmond Times*, July 23, 1891--this edition is from *Southern Historical Society Papers*, XIX (1891), pp. 324-326. **Page 182**: The coat *was* in Scotland. Mary Anna gave it to a Scottish Presbyterian minister in 1868. It was returned to her years later and she kept it until her death in 1915. In 1926 her granddaughter Julia Christian Preston presented it to VMI. **Page 183**: This poem is from *Southern Historical Society Papers*, X (1882), pp. 76-78. **Page 185**: This photograph of Julia Jackson has rarely, if ever, been published before, though other poses apparently from the same sitting (same dress, etc.) are known. **Page 186**: Henry Kyd Douglas, I RODE WITH STONEWALL (see endnote for page 61 above), p. 230. **Page 188**: *Southern Historical Society Papers*, XXV (1897), p. 112. **Back Cover**: This statue of Jackson by John Henry Foley (of England), located in Richmond, Virginia, was dedicated October 26, 1875; the quotation is from Lyle (see endnote for page xxxviii above), p. 320.

INDEX

A. Hoen & Co., 29
Alabama,
  Fourth (4th) Alabama Regiment, 50-51
Allen, Lt. Col., 152 (portrait)
Anderson, Richard Heron (CSA general), 139
Andrews, William H., 83
Antietam (Maryland), Battle of (also Sharpsburg), xxxiv, 90, 118, 121, 123 (map), 177
Appomattox, 51, 118, 132, 178, 186
Army of Northern Virginia, 27, 32, 34, 36, 72, 85
Army of the Shenandoah, 27, 29, 42, 44
Arnold, Laura Jackson (younger sister), 3
Ashby, Turner (CSA colonel), 35, 77, 91, 183
Ashby's Gap, Virginia, 40, 41, 42
Asheville, North Carolina, xxx
Augusta, Georgia, 118, 119
Austin, Texas, 77

Baltimore, Maryland, xxvii, xxix
Baltimore and Ohio Rail Road, 118, 199
Banks, Nathaniel Prentice (Union general), xxii, 36, 61, 71, 77, 78, 80, 81, 82, 90, 95, 99
Barclay, Alexander Tedford ("Ted"), xxvii, 145, 159
Barksdale's Mississippians, xxxii (illus.)
Battles and Leaders of the Civil War, xxviii, xxix, xxx
Beauregard, Pierre Gustave Toutant "P.G.T." (CSA general), xvi, 37 (portrait), 44, 66, 183
Bee, Barnard Elliott (CSA general), xvi, 49, 50, 66
Benson, Berry Greenwood, 118, 119 (illus.), 153
Berdan's Sharpshooters, 84 (illus.)
Blackford, Charles Minor, 55, 88, 195
Blackford, Charles Minor III, 55

Blackford, Susan Leigh, 55
Blackwood's Edinburgh Magazine, 125
Bloody Angle, xxxv, 77, 172
Blue Ridge, xix, 14, 40, 41, 65, 70, 80, 90
Bolivar Heights, (West) Virginia, 80
Boteler, Alexander Robinson, 56, 57
Botetourt County, Virginia, 11
Bowling Green, Kentucky, 13
Bowling Green, Virginia, 154, 159
Brady, Matthew, 24, 126, 192
Brandy Station, Virginia, 73, 77, 98
Bridgeford, Maj., 152 (portrait)
Bridgewater, Virginia, 80
Briscoe Station, Battle of (Virginia), 82
Brownsburg, Virginia, 56
Bryan, Joseph, 179
Buchanan, Virginia, 13
Bunker Hill, 125
Burnside, Ambrose Everett, 114, 123

Camden, Gideon Draper, 56
Camp Chase, 21
carte de visite, front cover (illus.), xxxvii, 46, 126, 191
Casler, John Overton, 161
Cedar Mountain (Virginia), Battle of (Cedar Run, Slaughter Mt.), 34, 72, 86, 88, 98, 99 (map)
Centerville (Centreville), Virginia, 58, 108, 109, 113
Century Magazine, xxix, 92
Chancellorsville, place and Battle of (Virginia), xv, xxi, xxix, xxxv, 30, 82, 133, 134-135 (map), 137, 139, 144, 145, 147, 151, 153, 154, 157, 158, 162, 163, 177, 179-180
Chantilly, Virginia, 75, 114
Chapultepec, Mexico, 3, 67, 83
Charleston Mercury, 49
Charlotte County, Virginia, 169
Charlottesville, Virginia, 181
Chestney, T.O. (CSA major), 94
Chickahominy River, 69, 71, 72, 95, 100
Churabusco, Mexico, 3
Charles Town, (West) Virginia, 36

202

Clarksburg, (West) Virginia, 3
Cobb, Thomas Reade Rootes (CSA general), xxviii, 119
Columbia, Tennessee, 62
Contreras, Mexico, 3, 67
Cooke, John Esten, 87, 195-197
Colston, Raleigh Edward (CSA general), 146
corps of cadets (see VMI)
Cowell, D.T., 191
Crenshaw's Farm, 98
Crutchfield, Stapleton (CSA colonel), 156
Cutshaw's Battery, 111
Cross Keys, Battle of (Virginia), 81, 82, 95, 184
Culpepper County, Virginia, 86

Dabney, Dr. Robert Lewis, 56, 152 (portrait)
Dam No. 5, 35, 194
Davidson College, 5
Davis, Jefferson, 76
Delaplane, Virginia (see Piedmont, Virginia)
Douglas, Henry Kyd, 152 (portrait), 186-187, 197, 200
Drecke, D.M., 133

Early, Jubal Anderson (CSA general), xxiv, 100, 186
Edmonds, Amanda Virginia, 42
Elzey, Arnold (CSA general), 94, 166
Ewell, Richard Stoddert (CSA general), 37 (portrait), 62, 72, 109, 132, 183

Fairfield, Virginia, 22
Fayetteville, North Carolina, 172
Field's Brigade, xxix, 98
Field's Division, 13
First Brigade (see Stonewall Brigade)
First Manassas (Virginia), Battle of (also First Bull Run), 40, 41, 44, 45, 48 (map), 49, 51, 52, 54, 65, 69, 70, 118, 161, 184
First National Flag ("Stars and Bars"), 60 (illus.)
Fluvanna County, Virginia, 179

Foley, John Henry, 210
"foot cavalry," 24, 73, 92, 95, 107 (illus.), 115, 116, 118
Fort Delaware, 21
Fort Monroe (Virginia), 114
Fort Sumter (South Carolina), 7, 19, 118, 161
Franklin, Battle of (Virginia), 77
Franklin, (West) Virginia, 80
Franklin's US Corps, 133
Frederick County, Virginia, 161
Fredericksburg, Battle of (Virginia), xxviii, xxx, xxxii, 33, 66, 124, 134-135 (map), 157, 184
Fredericksburg, Virginia, 33, 66, 124, 133, 137, 139, 154, 157, 166
Fremont, John Charles (Union general), 22, 61, 77, 78, 80, 81
Front Royal, Battle of (Virginia), 77, 80, 81, 95

Gaines' Mill (Virginia), Battle of (also First Cold Harbor or the Chickahominy), 79, 94
Gainsboro, Virginia, 161
Galt, Alexander, 56, 57
Garrick's Ford, 184
Georgia, 83, 118, 121
  First (1st) Georgia Regulars, 83
  Eleventh (11th) Georgia Volunteer Regiment, 121
Gettysburg, Pennsylvania (place and Battle of), xxix, 162, 172, 177, 178, 184
Glendale Crossroads, Virginia, vi
Goochland County, Virginia, 179
Gordon, John Brown (CSA general), 186
Gordonsville, Virginia, 132
Goshen Pass, Virginia, xxi
Greeley, Horace, 161
Greenbriar River, 21
Gregg, Maxcy (CSA general), 33
Guillaume, Lewis Mathieu Didier, frontispiece, 160, 191
Guinea Station, Virginia, 161, 165 (photograph), 172

Hagerstown, Maryland, 186
Haigh, Charles Thomas, 172-173, 173 (photograph), 196

203

Hamburg, South Carolina, 118
Hamilton's Crossing, Virginia, 133, 145, 154, 155
Hampden-Sydney College, 139, 169
Hannah, Samuel Baldwin, 169-170
Hanover Court House, Virginia, 132
Harman, John (CSA major), 34, 61, 62, 197
Harper's Ferry, Virginia, 23, 26, 28, 36, 73, 120, 123, 163
Harper's Monthly, 76
Harper's Publishing Company, xxix
Harrisonburg, Virginia, 80
Harrison's Landing at Berkeley Plantation, Virginia, 93
Hawks, Wells Joseph (CSA major), 152 (portrait), 163 (mention and portrait)
Hayes, Rutherford Birchard (Union officer and later 19th US president), xxiv
Hays, Harry Thompson (CSA general), 183
Healey, Robert (CSA lieutenant), 103
Henry House, 66
Henry, O. (William Sydney Porter), xxx
Hill, Ambrose Powell "A.P." (CSA general), xxix, 37 (portrait), 72 (mention and portrait), 75, 91, 93, 95, 98, 103, 123, 139, 146, 148, 156, 163
Hill, Daniel Harvey (CSA general), 94
Hillsboro Military Academy, 172
Hillsboro, (West) Virginia, 21
Hoge, Moses Drury (Reverend), 32
Hollins, George Nichols (CSN commodore), 181
Hollywood Cemetery (Richmond, Virginia), 167
Holt, David Eldred, 85, 136
Hooker, Joseph (Union general), 82, 123, 133, 137, 138, 139, 144, 157
Hotchkiss, Jedediah (CSA topological engineer), 23, 81, 152 (portrait)
Horse Shoe Salient, 132
Houdon, Jean A., xxiv
Howard, Oliver Otis, 134, 137, 139, 158
Hunter, Alexander, 101
Hunter, David (Union general), xxiv
Huntersville, (West) Virginia, 21

Illustrated London News, The, 46, 126, 128
Isbell, Bob, 88

Jackson, Cummins (uncle), 3
Jackson, Elinor "Ellie" Junkin (first wife), 5, 6 (portrait), 43
Jackson, Elizabeth (older sister), 3
Jackson, infant son, 5
Jackson, Jonathan (father), 3
Jackson, Julia (daughter), 5, 161, 185 (photograph)
Jackson, Julia (mother), 3
Jackson, Mary Anna "Anna" Morrison (second wife), xxii, 5, 8 (mention and portrait), 41-42, 68, 161, 170, 173, 185, 192
Jackson, Mary Graham (infant daughter), 5
Jackson, Thomas Jonathan "Stonewall,"
  at Antietam: 123
  biography of: 3-10
  burial of: xxi, 164-168, 169-170, 172-173, 200
  burial of amputated arm, xvi
  at Cedar Run (Cedar Mountain, Slaughter Mountain): 34, 72-73, 86-87, 88-89, 98, 99
  at Chancellorsville: 133, 134-135, 151, 154-159
  at Chantilly: 75
  compassion of: 30-31, 33, 36-38, 163
  confidence in on part of troops: 51, 58-60, 73, 76, 85, 89, 95, 104
  criticism of: 52, 62, 63-64, 75, 97, 100, 153
  death of: 159, 161-168, 172-173, 177
  demeanor of: 17, 39, 51, 53, 55, 63, 66, 67-69, 71, 89, 97, 116, 117, 125-127, 144
  and discipline: 62-63, 76, 122
  and duty: v, 7, 15, 69, 75, 129, 164
  early childhood of: 3
  evoked in a prayer, xvi
  at Gaines' Mill (First Cold Harbor): 94

as horseman, 63, 197-198
at Jackson's Mill: 3
at McDowell: 77-80
at First Manassas: 48, 69
at Fredericksburg: 33, 56, 134
at Harper's Ferry: 27-28
headquarters of: xxv (illus. of Winchester),
illustrations of:
  Jackson as First Lieutenant in Mexico (1847), 2
  Boteler sketch (1862) 57
  Brady portrait (1851), 24
  Fredericksburg portrait (1863)
  Galt sketch (1862), 57
  "General Thomas Jackson" (engraved from Winchester photograph), 9
  Guillaume engraving (Jackson on horse), 160
  Guillaume portrait, frontispiece
  "Jackson at 24 (1848)," 4
  "Jackson's Staff," 152
  Julio painting (1869), 143
  "Major Thomas Jackson," 6
  Nast engraving, 174
  "Professor T.J. Jackson" (1855 photograph), xxxviii
  Reinhart portrait (1862), 46
  Sheppard engraving of Lee and Jackson, 140
  statue at Manassas, 51
  statue in Lexington, 187
  statue in Richmond, back cover
  "Southern Generals," 37
  Winchester photograph (1862), xxxvii
  engraving from Winchester photograph, 130
  woodcut portrait from English newspaper (1862), 126
  woodcut portrait from English newspaper (1863), 128
  "Wounded," 147
  "Wounding of Jackson," 150
  Volck drawing (1861), 53
leaves for war: 19, 21-23
in Lexington: 7, 11-12, 39
at Malvern Hill: 31, 83
marriages of: 5
in the Mexican War: 3, 16, 67, 83
military strategies of: xxii, 36, 41, 42, 43, 44, 49, 63-64, 70-72, 77-82, 88-89, 94, 99, 105, 107-109, 121-122, 123, 133, 134, 139-141, 144, 145-149, 151, 154-159, 162, 176, 177, 198
nicknames for: vi, xxxv, 15, 16, 23, 37, 48, 49, 50, 52, 64, 66, 70, 75, 85, 90, 91, 97, 115, 121, 136
personality of: 12, 30-31, 33-35, 55, 57, 66-69, 71, 73-77, 82, 9, 11, 57, 116, 117, 127
photographs of: xxxvii, xxxviii, 2, 4, 24, 191
physical appearance (including dress) of: 11, 16, 29-30, 29, 53, 63, 73, 83, 89, 97, 104, 116, 117, 125-127, 137-138, 142, 144
at Port Republic: 35
quoted: xviii, 19, 27, 29, 30, 32, 33, 34, 35, 36, 38, 39, 41-42, (in letter), 48, 49, 75, 133, 136, 144, 151, 163
and religious aspects of his life: 7, 15, 30, 38, 66, 87, 97, 127
at Romney: 62-64
at Second Manassas: 36-37, 76, 99, 114
sleeping habits of: 31-33, 54, 55, 56
tastes of: (in food and whiskey) 35, 61; (liking for lemons and other sour things), 61, 196-197

Union attitudes and opinions toward: v, 73, 86-87, 89, 94, 120, 124, 133, 153
at VMI: xxi, 5, 15-16, 66, 68, 97, 169-170
at West Point: 3, 67
at Winchester: 36
and wounding (at Chancellorsville): 135, 137, 148, 151, 153, 156, 159, 178-179
Jackson, Warren (older brother), 3
Jackson's Corps (see Second Corps)
Jackson's Mill, 3
James River, 93
Johnson, Bradley Tyler (CSA general), xxxi
Johnson, Edward "Alleghany" (CSA general), 80
Johnston, Albert Sidney (CSA general), 37 (portrait)
Johnston, Joseph Eggleston (CSA general), 29, 54, 66, 69
Jones, Meriwhether, 191

205

Junkin, Elinor (see Jackson, Elinor)
Junkin, George (Reverend), xx, 5
Julio, E.B.D., 143 (painting by)

Kearny, Philip (Union general), 112-113
Kentucky, 122
Kernstown, Virginia, and Battle of, xx, 77, 80, 81
Kershaw, Joseph Brevard (CSA general), xxviii
Koontz, George W., 154-159

Lacy, James Horace (CSA major), 179
Lane's Brigade, 172
Lee, Fitzhugh (CSA general and R.E. Lee's nephew), 144, 177, 200
Lee, "Light Horse" Harry (R.E. Lee's father), xxi
Lee Memorial Chapel, xxi, 11
Lee, Robert Edward (CSA general), xvi, xx, xxi, xxii, xxiii, 13, 27, 33, 89, 115, 119, 132, 137-138, 139-141, 140 (portrait), 142, 143 (portrait), 157, 162, 164, 169, 177, 178, 181, 182, 183, 200
Letcher, John (Governor of Virginia), xx, xxiv, 28, 56
Lewis, Jim (Jackson's servant in camp), 31, 32, 38, 97-98
Lexington Gazette, 43, 129
Lexington, Virginia, xviii (mention and photograph), xxi, xxiii, xxiv, xxvii, 5, 7, 10 (mention and photograph), 11, 13, 14, 19, 21, 22, 26, 27, 39, 43, 58, 68, 97, 143, 145, 167, 168, 169, 170, 171, 172, 179, 181, 186, 187, 188
Liberty Hall Volunteers (LHV), 11, 21, 38, 58, 59, 129, 145, 195
Lincoln, Abraham (16th US President), xx, 13, 19, 76
Louisiana Tiger, 137 (illus.)
Long, Andrew Davidson, xxvii, 77, 137
Long, James D., 157
Long, Theodore S., xxiv
Long, Walter E., 77
Longstreet, James "Pete" (CSA general), xxviii, 13, 32, 37 (portrait), 76, 91, 98, 99, 113, 114
Louisiana Pelicans, 110-111, 110 (illus.)
Lynchburg, Virginia, 55, 88, 167, 200
Lyle, John Newton, xxvii, xxxviii, 8, 11, 21, 26, 39, 41, 42, 51, 52, 53, 61, back cover

McClellan, George Brinton (Union general), xxii, 3, 31, 69, 70, 71, 93, 99, 114,
McCormick, Cyrus H., xix-xx
McDowell, Battle of (Virginia), 77, 80, 81, 82, 95, 132, 172
McDowell, Irvin (Union general), xxii, 71, 80
McGuire, Hunter Holmes (Doctor and CSA officer), xxvii, 20, 27-29, 28 (portrait), 144, 152 (portrait), 188
McIntosh's Battalion, 154
McKinley, William (Union officer and 24th US president), xxiv
McLaws, Lafayette (CSA general), 139

Magruder, John Bankhead (CSA general), 67
Maine, xv, 153
Malvern Hill, Battle of (Virginia), 31, 83, 84, 92, 184
Manassas Junction, Virginia, 40, 45, 106, 113
Manassas, Battles of (see First and Second Manassas)
Mansfield, Joseph King Fenno (Union general), 123
Marye's Heights, xxx
Maryland, xxxiv, 114, 121, 122, 186
First (1st) Maryland Cavalry, xxix
Maryland Heights, 80
Massanutton, 184
Maury Grays, the, 62
Maury, Matthew Fontaine ("Pathfinder of the Sea"), xxi
Maximilian, Emperor of Mexico, xxi, 3

206

Mexican War, the, xxi, 2, 3, 16 67, 71, 82, 83
Middlesex Southrons, the, xxix, 65
Miley, Michael, 10, 18, 26
Milroy, Robert Huston (Union general), 78, 80, 81
Minnis Gallery, 191
Mississippi
  Sixteenth (16th) Mississippi Regiment, 85, 136
Missouri, 161, 186
Moffett (or "Moffatt"), George Henry, 21
Monroe, James (5th US president), 167
Montgomery, Alabama, 60
Montgomery, Walter A., 132, 136, 178
Moore, Edward A., 13
Morgan, John Hunt (CSA general), 122, 199
Morrison, Mary Anna (see Mary Anna Jackson)
Morrison, Joseph Graham (CSA captain), 152 (portrait), 200
Mosby's Partisan Rangers, 179

Nast, Thomas, 201

New Market, Battle of (Virginia), xxiv
New Orleans, Louisiana, 183, 185
Newton, Virginia, 37
New York, New York, xxvii, xxxi, 24
New York Times, 90
New York Tribune, 90
North Carolina
  Thirty-seventh (37th) North Carolina Cavalry, 172
  Twelfth (12th) North Carolina Regiment, 132, 133
  Eighteenth (18th) North Carolina Regiment, vi
  Forty-fourth (44th) North Carolina Regiment, 156

Obenchain, William Alexander, 13
Ogden College, 13
Oklahoma, 161
Orange Court House, Virginia, 98

Owen, William Miller (CSA lieutenant), xxx
Oxford University, England, 76

Palmer, John Williamson, 90
Paris, Virginia, 40, 41-43
Pamunkey River, 92
Pendleton, Alexander Swift "Sandie" (CSA colonel), 31, 34, 152 (portrait)
Pennsylvania, 122, 186
  Twelfth (12th) Pennsylvania Cavalry, 107
Petersburg, Battle of (Virginia), 86
Peterson, Dennie Donald (USMC lieutenant), v
Piedmont Station, Virginia, 40, 42, 45
Poague, William, 62
Pochantas County, Virginia, 21
Pope, John (Union general), 72, 74, 76, 86, 91, 98, 99, 105, 107, 114
Portland, Oregon, 21
Port Republic, Battle of (Virginia), 35, 81, 82, 95
Potomac Guards, the, 161
Potomac River, xxxiv, 35, 85
Powhatan County, Virginia, 179
Preston, John Thomas Lewis (CSA officer), 15, 41, 43-44
Preston, Margaret "Maggie" (sister-in-law), 43
Preston, William Caruthers "Willie," 36, 38, 43, 194
Pulaski Guards, the, xxxv, 35

Randolph, J.W., 90
Rapidan River, 73, 74, 99
Rappahannock River, xxxi, 69, 71, 73, 80, 82, 98, 99, 133, 137, 145, 184
Redwood, Allen Christian, xxxvi (photograph), xxxvii-xxxiii, 65, 74, 92, 102, 106, 110, 142, 143, 176
Redwood, Henry, xxxiii
Reinhart, Benjamin Franklin, 46
Rice's Battery, 154
Richmond Dispatch, The, 27
Richmond, Virginia, xx, xxi, xxii, xxiii, xxxv, 13, 19, 22, 23, 29,

207

31, 32, 69, 77, 90, 92, 93, 98, 108, 114, 136, 163, 164, 167, 169, 172
Robins, William M., 50
Rockbridge Artillery, the, 62, 139
Rockbridge Baths, Virginia, 77
Rockbridge Rifles, the, 19
Rockingham County, Virginia, xix, 145
Rodes, Robert Emmett (CSA general), 144, 158, 200
Routzahn Gallery, xxxvii

St. Louis, Missouri, 186
St. Paul, Minnesota, 21
Salem Church, Virginia, 135
Salem, North Carolina, 5
"Scabbard Speech," 17-19, 192-193
Scott, Winfield (Union general), 67
Scribner's Monthly, xxix, 92
Second Corps, Army of Northern Virginia (Jackson's Corps), xxix, xxxiv, 72, 96, 139, 148, 155, 158, 162, 164, 170
Second Manassas (also Second Bull Run), Battle of (Virginia), 23, 36, 43, 60, 75, 76, 92, 99, 105, 108, 184
Second National Flag ("Stainless Banner"), 168 (illus.), 173
Seven Days' Fight (Seven Days' Battle, Battle of Seven Days), 23, 32, 92, 98, 132
Sharpsburg (see Antietam),
Shenandoah River, 40, 41, 90
Shenandoah Valley ("the Valley"), xix, xx, xxii, xxiv, xxv, xxxiii, 5, 19, 30, 52, 58, 62, 63, 65, 69, 71, 72, 76, 77, 78-79 (map), 79, 80, 81, 82, 83, 90, 99, 105, 132, 167, 186, 188
Shepherdstown, (West) Virginia, 186
Sheppard, W.L., 140
Sheridan, Philip Henry (Union general), xxiv, xxv, 181
Shields, James (Union general), 61, 78, 80, 81, 82
Slaughter Mountain (see Cedar Mountain)
Smith, James Power (CSA officer), 61, 139-141, 152 (portrait)
Smith, Francis Henney (superintendent of VMI), 169, 170
South Carolina
    First (1st) South Carolina Volunteers, 118
South River, 80
Spotsylvania County, Virginia, 179
Spotsylvania [Court House] (also "Spottsylvania"), 77, 132, 145, 172
Staunton, Virginia, xxiii, 22-23, 62, 68, 77
Stevensburg ("Stephensby"), Virginia, 98
Stone Bridge, 113
Stonewall Brigade (First Brigade, Army of the Shenandoah), v, xxxv, 11, 27, 35, 41-43, 48, 50-51, 52, 58, 65, 77, 80, 87, 89, 90, 91, 129, 145, 148, 151, 161, 163, 173, 184
"Stonewall Jackson's Guard," 11
Stonewall Jackson's Way (song), 75, 90
Strasburg, Virginia, xix
Stuart, James Ewell Brown "Jeb" (CSA general),37 (portrait), 91, 137, 138, 139, 142, 146, 148, 162, 183
Sudley Church, Virginia, 111
Sumner, Edwin Vose (Union general), 123

Taylor, Richard "Dick" (CSA general), 62
Tennessee, 62
    First (1st) Tennessee Regiment, 62
Terry, William (CSA general), 148, 191
Texas, 11, 77
Thompson, James, 121
Thoroughfare Gap, Virginia, 105
Townsend, Mary Ashley, 183
Trimble, Isaac Ridgeway (CSA general), 33-34, 85, 100
Tyler, John (10th US president), 60, 167
Tyler, Letitia, 60

208

Valentine, Edward, xxi, 27, 188
Valley Campaign, xxii, 23, 72, 76, 78, 81, 95, 97
Valley Pike, xxv, 26, 30, 77
Vance, Zebulon (CSA general), 191
Vera Cruz, Mexico, 67
Virginia Medical College, 27
Vicksburg, Mississippi, 172
Virginia
    Second (2nd) Virginia Cavalry, 55
    Eleventh (11th) Virginia Cavalry, 21, 161
    Fourteenth (14th) Virginia Cavalry, 169
    Nineteenth (19th) Virginia Cavalry, 11
    First (1st) Virginia Regiment, 166
    Second (2nd) Virginia Regiment, 27, 28, 186
    Fourth (4th) Virginia Regiment, xxxv, 11, 58, 59, 129, 145-149
    Fifth (5th) Virginia Regiment, 77
    Thirty-third (33rd) Virginia Regiment, 161
    Fifty-fifth (55th) Virginia Regiment, 65, 92-116, 156
Virginia Military Institute, xxi, xxxv, 5, 7, 11, 12, 13, 14 (illus.), 17, 18 (photograph), 19, 20, 22, 66, 67 (photograph), 97, 121, 130, 167, 169, 171, 172, 179, 181; CORPS OF CADETS, xxiv, 12, 13, 17, 19, 20 (photograph), 22-23, 66, 97, 121, 167, 171 (photograph) 172; JACKSON MEMORIAL HALL, 191
Vizetelly, Frank, 128
Volck, Adelbert J., 53, 195

Wales, the Prince and Princess of, 76
Walker, James Alexander (CSA general), xxvii, xxxv, 191, 193
Walker, Reuben Lindsay (CSA general), 34
Walker, William Henry (CSA general), 119, 199
Warrenton, North Carolina, 132

Warrenton Springs, Virginia, 100
Washington Artillery, the, xxx
Washington College (Washington & Lee University), xx, xxi, xxiv, 5, 11, 21, 26 (mention and photograph), 58, 59
Washington, D.C., xx, xxiv, 21, 162
Washington, George, xxiv, xxv, 167
Waterloo Bridge, 103
Watkins, Sam R., 62-64
West Point (US Military Academy), 3, 5, 13, 49, 67, 73, 121
West Virginia, 3, 21, 138, 161, 169, 186
Wharton, H.M., 86
Wheeling, (West) Virginia, 21
White House, the, 92
White, Hugh Augustus, 58, 59 (photograph)
White, James J., 58
William S. (Reverend Doctor), 22, 58, 170
White's Ford, Virginia, xxxiv
Wilderness, the, Battle of (Virginia), 132, 172, 181, 184
Wilkinson County, Mississippi, 85
Wilkinson Rifles, the, 85
Winchester, Battle[s] of (Virginia), xxiii, 36, 77, 80, 81, 82, 95
Winchester, Virginia, xxiii, xxv, xxxvii, 27, 36, 40, 41, 42, 59, 63, 80, 81 (map), 85, 125, 161
Winder, Charles Sidney (CSA general), 35, 62, 89
Wolfe, Thomas, xxxiii
Wolseley, Viscount Garnet Joseph, 125
Woodville, Mississippi, 85

Yerby House, 33, 191, 194
Yorktown, Virginia, 69